The SEASON of the CICADAS

Published by Mindstir Media, LLC

45 Lafayette Rd | Suite 181| North Hampton, NH 03862 | USA

1.800.767.0531 | www.mindstirmedia.com

Printed in the United States of America

ISBN-13: 978-0-9985781-4-9

Library of Congress Control Number: 2017900224

The SEASON of the CICADAS

written by
LESTER WAYNE DANIELS JR.

MINDSTIR MEDIA

This book is dedicated to the memory of Ross E. Hutchins and Arvis L. Stewart.

TABLE OF CONTENTS

I

PREFACE

I've been infatuated with the cicada since I was a young boy. I've always remembered the hot summers listening to their songs during the height of the day. My first recollection of the cicada was at the approximate age of 5 when I discovered an empty shell on the side of my neighbor's tree. When I plucked the shell from the trunk, it crumbled into dust. I was truly puzzled at the time.

Later in grade school, my home room teacher gave us a class project. It was September and she wanted us to go out and gather insects for "show and tell." One of the insects listed was the cicada. I was more into art and line drawings than hunting for bugs at this age.

Midway into October the same year, I found a dead annual cicada clinging to a leaf that had fallen to the sidewalk. Excited, I tried to pick it up. The cicada's body fell into pieces since it was dried out and dead for some time. I was very disappointed but with a heightened curiosity.

We had a small school library where I enjoyed our class visits. While browsing literature on dinosaurs, I located a book with some excellent line art entitled "The Cicada;" the author being the late, Ross E. Hutchins. I picked the book up mainly for the pictures that was illustrated by the late, Arvis L. Stewart. Since the book was easy reading, I decided to peruse it and was so intrigued by the subject matter, I became obsessed with the cicada and determined to see one!

It was July the following year when the cicadas began to sing again. I was very enthusiastic and eager to hunt. I would climb into my neighbor's trees where the cicadas were singing and would wait. I watched very patiently until a male cicada landed on a nearby branch. The insect was busy striking notes and oblivious to my presence. The cicada would sing a little and start walking towards me. He would then stop, sing, and approach some more. The cicada kept inching closer and closer until he finally came within my range. Then POW! I caught the critter with my bare hands and the unsuspecting cicada didn't like it one bit! The cicada gave off a loud nonstop screeching sound that attracted the attention of my neighbors. I climbed down from the tree with my prize and took him to show my mother. I was a very happy young lad. I later let the cicada go and would continue the hunt for many more.

Every summer, the cicadas would come and I would be waiting. It would be a long time before I got to see an actual 17 year cicada but the annual cicadas held me over until then... Everyone has their humble beginnings.

My full name is Lester Wayne Daniels Jr.... I grew up in Northern Ohio where I graduated from Bowling Green State University with a degree in criminal justice. I still live in the great state of Ohio with my family where I continue to independently study nature and natural history. I enjoy traveling, hiking, camping, and outdoor adventuring. I also have interests in paleontology and macro photography. Besides the cicada, I have a fondness for another unique insect that is common to most people as the "praying" mantis.

AUTHOR'S NOTE: No cicadas were injured or destroyed for the construction of this book!

II
ACKNOWLEDGEMENTS

I would like to thank my wife, Sarah, and our children, Michael & Victoria, for tolerating my insect fetishes; my mother for raising me abnormal; Dan "Century" Mozgai of Cicada Mania for creating the best site on the web;" Gene Kritsky for being my friend and inspiration for writing this thing; John Cooley, David Marshall, & Chris Simon for their continued hard work in cicada pioneering; Adam Fleishman for all of the great cicada taxidermy; James P. Key & Max S. Moulds for acquiring some of my needed specimens; Roy Troutman for putting together some excellent sound recordings and being a true cicada enthusiast; the late Charles L. Marlatt & Charles V. Riley for setting the stage that many of us follow; the late Ross E. Hutchins; and Arvis L. Stewart for their life long influences; Our Lady of the Pines & the Sorrowful Mother Shrine for granting me continued access to their beautiful properties, and many thanks to the following... Ohio Department of Natural Resources, the Ohio State Park System, Fremont Police Chief Dean Bliss & the City of Fremont, the management of Findley State Park, Ashland County Park District, Basilica and National Shrine of Our Lady of Consolation, Five Rivers Metroparks, Lorain County Metroparks, Summit Metroparks, Cleveland Metroparks, Cuyahoga Valley National Park, Columbus & Franklin County Metroparks, Rogers-Lakewood Park, Rutherford B. Hayes Presidential Center & Spiegel Grove State Park; Sandusky County Park District, Spring Grove Cemetery, Washtenong Memorial Park, everyone who participated in the on-going mapping projects; those universities involved with their continued research, and last but not least... to the cicadas for simply being themselves!

III
INTRODUCING
THE CICADA

"Swamp cicada" Neotibicen tibicen tibicen

Bugs, insects, bugs, insects, bugs, bugs, and more bugs….. Love them or hate them, they are an intricate part of just about every food chain across the world. No matter where you live or try to hide, most likely some form of insect will be lurking by. There's really no escaping them. Their diversity is complex and with some, their savagery has no equal. They've been around for millions of years and are some of the planet Earth's oldest living organisms. They were here long before us and will likely be here long after we're gone. The more one is willing to accept and appreciate their inevitable existence, the happier one's peace of mind will become.

Among these creatures that far out-number us, one in particular likes to be the center of attention. There comes a time when the summer sun reaches its peak across the nearby woodlands and a sudden call breaks apart the normal clatter of animals going about their daily lives. The audible sound is loud and can carry a great distance! You know then the days have become hot and the smaller plants have withered and succumbed to the heat. The sound is distinct and for many farmers, they know the harvest will soon be upon them. After hearing the first, more of their kin begins to follow suite and create audible sounds of their own. When many more join in, it becomes near impossible to hear the birds chirping or the squirrels running through the brittle grasses. It is now the season of the cicadas. They are an insect that is so often heard but rarely seen. Yet, most people are familiar with them and their presence is unavoidable.

So what is a cicada? They are horrible plant sucking pestilence that hide underground and wait for some poor soul to drag under who inadvertently stumble upon their lair! No, no, no…. That is what some people would like you to believe but they fit none of that description…. Within the next few chapters, I hope you come to endear this creature that has mesmerized me for most of my existence!

Let's start with some science. Cicadas, pronounced in Northern dialect as "suh-kay-duhs," belong to the phylum Arthropoda and the class Insecta (or insects) which are those creatures described as having three body parts (head, thorax, & abdomen), two antennae, and six legs. The name originated around the 14th century from a Latin word meaning "tree cricket." Cicadas belong to the insect order called the Hemiptera and the suborder Auchenorrhyncha (formerly Homoptera) which are classified as those insects with piercing mouth parts designed for sucking plant juices and having three stages of development (egg, nymph, & adult). Cicadas are the largest insects in their order and are closely related to aphids and scale insects. Cicadas make up a super family called the Cicadoidea which also includes leaf and tree hoppers, and are in their own family called the Cicadidae. From there, the Cicadidae is broken down into groups called the "genus." Three of the genera that exist near the Great Lakes are listed in this chapter. Genera are then broken further into each individual species...There are approximately 1300 species in the Cicadidae family, most of which are tropical. Only approximately 170 of these species inhabit North America. Several different species are described in this book. "Whew." I hope I didn't lose anybody after digesting all of that!

Worldwide, cicadas are heralded in folklore and myths and are often associated with "rebirth" in other cultures. Cicadas have a wide diversity and vary profoundly. There are species the size of fruit flies while others have wingspans over eight inches, like the species "Megapomponia imperatoria" that is found in Malaysia. Most known cicada species have multiyear life cycles. Some have developed "periodical" life cycles and are not seen for many years at a time; such as the Magicicadas.....

The cicadas living near the Great Lakes region are well known for their mating calls. Each species have their own unique songs and can be identified by the sounds they create. Only the males are able to produce sound by vibrating two membranes on their hollow abdomens. Female abdomens are full of eggs and have no sound producing organs.

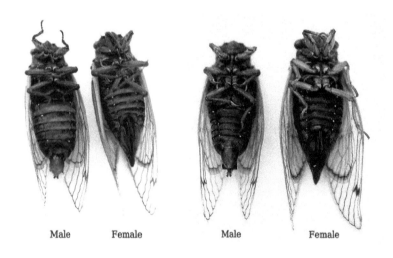

Gender comparisons
(Magicicada septendecim: Left) (Magicicada cassini: Right)

Male   Female   Male   Female

When males sing in unison, the noise can often deter predators and become deafening to the human ear. In some cases, especially in Magicicada species (see below), their calls can reach volumes of over a hundred decibels. Ouch! Decibels exceeding 85 can actually damage your ear drum after prolonged exposure! Ear plugs are sometimes recommended!

Cicadas are harmless to people and animals. They do not bite, sting, or carry diseases.

Here are some common genera found around the Great Lakes region. This isn't a complete list but is those familiar to me and covered in this book.

1. Genus Magicicada –

"Periodical cicada" Magicicada cassini

The "magic" cicada as they are sometimes referred since they "magically" appear out of the ground by the millions, are perhaps the most famous cicadas in the world. The Magicicada or "periodical cicada" became known by the first settlers to North America after they had mistaken them for a Biblical plague of locusts due to their large numbers... Hence the commonly used term "locusts" has forever been labeled not only to this genus, but the entire Cicadidae family. 17 year or 13 year locust is a popular alias. A more comical moniker given to this genus is "Satan's parakeets."

Periodical cicadas are found only in the Eastern United States. Up north, the genus requires 17 years to mature while in some Southern states, they require 13 years. There has been some dispute among entomologists whether there are six species or three species of Magicicada in the past. There are currently three recognized 17 year races (M. septendecim; aka: "Linnaeus' 17-year cicada," M. cassini; aka: "Cassin's 17-year cicada" or "dwarf cicada," M. septendecula: aka: "little 17-year cicada") and four 13 year races (M. tredecim; aka: "Riley's 13-year cicada," M. tredecassini; aka: "Cassin's 13-year cicada," M. tredecula; aka: "little 13-year cicada," and M. neotredecim; aka: "cryptic 13-year cicada"). These individual races coexist and live in synchronized harmony among their respective 13 or 17 year cycles but may prefer different habitations and flora.

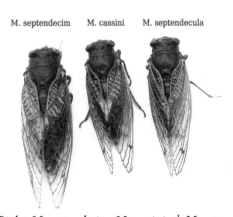

M. septendecim   M. cassini   M. septendecula

Left to Right: M. septendecim, M. cassini, & M. septendecula
Species comparison dorsal view

M. septendecim   M. cassini   M. septendecula

Left to Right: M. septendecim, M. cassini, & M. septendecula
Species comparison ventral view

Periodical cicada emergences are labeled as broods arranged with Roman numerals from Brood I to Brood XXX. Brood I through Brood XVII is designated to the 17 year races while Broods XVIII through XXX is designated to the 13 year races. However, periodical cicadas can get off schedule and emerge a few years too early or a few years too late but in smaller numbers. This is called "straggling" which can make it hard to construct accurate maps of their emergence years and areas. Weather abnormalities can trigger straggling occurrences. Some broods have become extinct (Brood's XI and XXI) and there has been some debate whether or not a few had ever really existed. There are currently 12 known 17 year broods and 3 known 13 year broods.

There has also been much discussion and mystery surrounding the prime numbered years for emergence. It is believed the reason for prime number years is to avoid predation since no animal predator can sync up with long life cycle of the cicada. Some animal species thrive well during emergence years but their numbers later decline again when the cicadas are no longer available as an annual food source.

The broods are believed to have evolved during the ice age era where the insects had to remain dormant for longer periods. This longer dormancy was a result of lower seasonal temperatures, thus increasing their life span and causing the eventual dawn of their periodicity. Also during this period, individual species of periodical cicadas began to evolve and split from a common ancestor. Recent studies have shown that today's species are still evolving due to separation and living in isolated relict populations across much of their historical range.

Periodical cicadas are usually 1 to 1.5 inches in length and have bright red eyes with orange wing veins and legs. The eye color can be various shades of red from a bright cherry to a darker maroon. Their bodies are black but give off a navy blue aura under proper lighting. They also have a "W" shaped marking on their transparent anterior wings which an "urban legend" associates this as a prediction for war. Some species are larger and have wide orange ventral abdominal bands (M. decim spp.) while the smaller forms either have thin orange bands (M. decula spp.) or are completely black (M. cassini spp;).

Magicicada septendecim

Magicicada cassini

Magicicada septendecula

Occasionally, periodical cicadas lack their natural pigmentation and can have blue-grey or white eyes and wing veins. This abnormality is a genetic variation and is extremely rare.

Blue-grey eyed & red eyed periodic cicada comparison

Blue-grey eyed color morph

Blue-grey eyed color morph

Blue-grey eyed color morph

2. Genus Neotibicen -

"Annual cicada" Neotibicen tibicen tibicen

This is the common annual cicada which is seen during the heat of mid to late summer. This genus was formerly called Tibicen which recently changed to Neotibicen in 2015. The time underground for annual cicadas to reach maturity is unknown but is believed to require at least 2 years or more. Since annual cicada broods overlap, they are found every year.

Annual cicadas are larger than periodical cicadas with some species reaching a length of two inches or more. Annual cicadas generally have black bodies with greenish wing veins and markings. Annual cicadas are found throughout the Eastern United States.

There are several species near the Great Lakes region. Different species like to sing at different times of the day but can form chorusing centers where each specific song can be identified.

3. Genus Okanagana -

"Canadian Cicada" Okanagana canadensis

This genus is often mistaken for periodic cicadas in that they can also appear in great numbers in late spring. They are approximately 1.0 to 1.25 inches in length and have black and orange colored bodies with beige undersides. This genus is distributed in the Great Lakes region but is not as well-known as their periodical and annual cousins.

Some of these species are believed to be proto-periodical, meaning they can be seen every year but in some years they are abundant while others they are nearly absent. Like annual cicadas, the actual time they take to mature is unknown but the species Okanagana rimosa, "Say's Cicada," may have a life span up to 9 years...

"Canadian Cicada" Okanagana canadensis

"Say's Cicada" Okanagana rimosa

Annual cicada Neotibicen lyricen lyricen

IV
CICADA TIMELINE

A BRIEF HISTORY OF THE CICADA

163 to 145 Million Years Ago: Upper Jurassic period - The first known cicada ancestors in the fossil record.

10,000 BC: Cicadas are mentioned in the 3rd book of the Iliad by Homer.

1766 BC: Shang Dynasty - Cicadas are used in Chinese art.

1122 BC: Chou Dynasty - Jade cicadas are used in religious ritual burials as symbols of the soul.

560 BC: The fable of the "Cicada & the Ant" is told by the slave, Aesop the Phrygian.

500 BC: Cicadas are used in the artwork of ancient Greek coins.

332 BC: Cicadas are kept as pets by the ancient Greeks. They are also studied and described by the famous philosopher, Aristotle.

300 BC: Cicadas are used as figurines in Italian jewelry.

200 BC: India cicadas are mentioned in the Hindu Laws - "The Institutes of Manu."

100 BC: A cicada is depicted in a mosaic from Pompeii.

500 AD: Cicada exuvia are used as ingredients for Chinese herbal medicines.

735 AD: Chinese Emperor Hang Ts'ung regards cicadas as symbols of the passage from mortal life to a higher state.

1350 AD: The term "cicada" originates from the Latin language.

1633 AD: The first Magicicada emergence is documented in the new world after being encountered by the Plymouth Colony.

1650 AD: A cicada is observed being devoured by a mantis by swordsman Wang Lang. Lang creates the Mantis (Kung Fu) Fighting Style.

1666 AD: The Brood XIV emergence becomes the first published account of the Magicicada by H. Oldenberg.

1759 AD: Magicicada septendecim is recognized and named "Cicada septendecim" by Swedish Scientist, Carolus Linnaeus.

1764 AD: Superstitions of war become instituted with the Magicicada.

1775 AD: Thomas Jefferson noted Brood II in his "Garden Book," and documented their periodicity from previous years.

1812 AD: Dr. S. P. Hildreth of Ohio confirms the 17 year life cycle of the Northern Magicicada.

1825 AD: The genus name "Tibicen" is assigned to many of the dog-day cicadas by P.A. Latreille.

1851 AD: M. cassini (then Cicada cassini) is identified and named a separate species by Dr. J.C. Fisher. The name was in honor of John Cassin's field research.

1858 AD: Dr. D. L. Phares confirms the existence of a 13 year life cycle in southern Magicicadas.

1865 AD: U.S. Department of Agriculture Entomologist Charles V. Riley publishes his first cicada bulletin and continues his research for years until Charles L. Marlatt takes over the project.

1868 AD: The known Magicicada species is increased to 4 as 13 year M. tredecim are recognized and named separate from the 17 year races by Benjamin D. Walsh and Charles V. Riley.

1870 AD: Brood XXI is seen for the last time in Florida prior to its extinction.

1885 AD: Brood X is last recorded in Canada prior to its extinction in that country.

1889 AD: W.L. Distant begins to classify many families and species of cicada which become the focus of his life.

1898 AD: U.S. Department of Agriculture Entomologist Charles L. Marlatt begins to map and assign names to the different Magicicada broods.

1906 AD: W. L. Distant publishes his "Synonymic Catalogue of Homoptera: Cicadidae."

1907 AD: C.L. Marlatt redefines the brood areas and renames them to what we still use today.

1925 AD: The genus name "Magicicada" is assigned to the periodical cicada by William T. Davis.

1940 AD: The U.S. Department of Agriculture discontinues the brood mapping project due to the outbreak of World War II.

1953 AD: M. septendecula is field studied by D. J. Borror and C.R. Reese.

1954 AD: Brood XI is seen for the last time in Connecticut prior to its extinction.

1962 AD: Richard Alexander and Thomas E. Moore further describe the species M. septendecula and M. tredecula.

1976 AD: R.S. Soper publishes his study of the proto-periodicity of Okanagana rimosa, revealing this species to possibly have a 9 year life cycle.

1988 AD: Brood X is noted to have a major 1 year deceleration in Southern Ohio and Northern Kentucky. This is later discovered to be a 13 year Ohio-Kentucky Brood. (See below.)

1996 AD (March): The first Magicicada preserve is proposed in Hamden, Connecticut near Sleeping Giant Park by Yale University.

1996 AD (June): The web page "Cicada Mania" is launched by Dan "Century" Mozgai and becomes a renowned cicada information resource around the world.

1996 AD: Species Tibicen bermudiana is confirmed to be extinct from the Bermuda region due to the destruction of its host plants from blight and the introduction of invasive bird species. The last male individual was heard singing in the early 90's.

1998 AD: A new 13 year cicada species "M. neotredecim" is discovered by C. Simon, John Cooley, David Marshall, & A. P. Martin.

1998 AD (May): 17 year Brood IV and 13 year Brood XIX emerges together in Missouri and Iowa; a phenomenon that only occurs once every 221 years (17 X 13).

2000 AD: 1/100 of Brood X emerges 4 years ahead of schedule in parts of Southern Ohio which remains consistent in the past century and demonstrates evidence of a new brood that is evolving.

2001 AD: 13 year Magicicadas are hypothesized to be an independent Ohio-Kentucky Brood that went undiscovered for many years due to the overlapping emergence of other broods.

2013 AD: New Forest Cicada Project is established to determine the existence or extinction of the species Cicadetta montana from the New Forest in Britain.

2014 AD: The Ohio-Kentucky Brood is confirmed after a 13 year wait.

2015 AD: The North American Tibicen genus is re-categorized and renamed after intensive studies into their phylogenetics. Eastern North American species are now classified as Neotibicen while the Western North American species are now the Hadoa.

2016 AD: The new genus Gigatibicen is named which includes North America's largest cicada, Gigatibicen auletes, formerly called Neotibicen auletes and Megatibicen auletes.

V
THE PERIODICAL CICADA

LIFE CYCLE

The longevity of a cicada's life cycle is perhaps the one thing that draws them so much attention and curiosity. Some species, like most insects, consist of an annual life cycle while others, like those discussed in this book, can live between 2 and 17 years. The cicada goes through a process that is called an "incomplete" metamorphosis; meaning their life stages is simply egg, nymph, and adult and does not include a pupal stage. We'll begin this chapter by learning about their later life stage which brings so much attention to them.

GOING TOWARD THE LIGHT

What triggers immature cicadas called "nymphs" to emerge from the ground during the spring of the 17th year is still unknown. There are theories about the changing of season to season, which intermittently stops the flow of nutrients in plants, acts has an internal clock for the growing cicadas. The plants they feed upon, such as trees, cease activity during the winter months and start up again the following spring. A tree's seasonal growth ring that develops within its trunk helps scientists in determining the overall age of the plant itself. It is believed that cicadas use these seasonal patterns to alert them in knowing when it is their year to make themselves appear. The year during an emergence, host trees and plants may suffer some decline in their health and growth since the maturing underground nymphs are feeding more vigorously in preparation for their adult lives. Otherwise, the lasting effects of high densities of feeding cicadas are not normally apparent.

With periodical cicadas or Magicicadas, it has been well plotted over the past 200 years where and when they'll exactly emerge. This was accomplished thanks chiefly to the hard work of the late entomologist, Charles Lester Marlatt. 13 year cicadas in the Southern states will start emerging in late April to early May while the Northern 17 year species will begin to emerge in late May and early June. Changes in seasonal temperatures may offset these emergence times by several weeks.

Whatever the reason, weeks before emerging, the nymph will begin to tunnel toward the surface of the ground where it will build a water proof chamber. The chamber's walls will be completely compacted and smooth,

Cicada tunnels exposed

made possible by liquids secreted from the nymph's body. This keeps the rain out and prevents their structure from crumbling.

Periodical cicadas often construct a turret (also called a cone, hut, or chimney) that can extend as high as one to two inches above the surface with rare occurrences of exceeding six inches or more. Cicada nymphs will erect turrets to elude excessive ground moisture and are the only species known in North America to build these temporary dwellings. At this stage in life, one can see the evidence of an adult cicada ready to be born since their bright red eyes are clearly visible as are their well-developed wing buds on each side of their body. Two black spots on their prothorax materialize a few days before departing the ground.

Cicada chimneys

EMERGENCE and ECDYSIS

Of all the facets of a cicada's life, nothing gains more hype and notoriety than the sudden appearance of millions of insects seemingly erupting from the earth! When the soil temperatures reach approximately 64 degrees Fahrenheit at a depth of about 8 inches, they begin to emerge in a mass exodus. They first emerge from areas that receive the most sun. Soil exposed to sunlight has increases in ground temperatures quicker than those areas covered by shade.

Thousands emerge all at once, beginning in the evening before dusk and persisting late into the morning hours the following day. Very few emerge during the height of the day since the

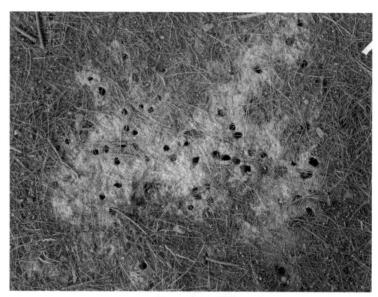

Emergence Holes

likelihood of being eaten by a predator greatly increases. Cicadas can number as many as 20,000 to 40,000 to a tree and up to 1.5 million an acre. Their overall weight is one of the largest biomasses on the planet! They leave behind half inch diameter emergence holes that actually help the soil since the departure of so many acts as a natural tilling. During a large emergence, the sounds they create while crawling through the leaf litter on the forest floor resemble that of rain hitting the ground.

Cicada nymph

The nymphs slowly walk in search of a sturdy support which will assist them in "molting" or casting off their final skin. Tree trunks, branches, flower stems, leaves, tall blades of grass, fence posts, and roadway signs are often used. Nymphs will even climb animals or a person's leg if they'll hold still long enough.

Once a support is selected, the nymphs will climb it as high as an inch or up to twenty feet from the ground until they are satisfied with a secure position. After fastening themselves to the bark with their legs, their skin will slowly split down their back or "mesothorax." The adult or "imago" cicada will begin this process called "ecdysis" or molting by first removing its back and head through muscle contractions. The body slowly follows as the cicada leans way back and dangle upside down from the opening made in its old skin. This old skin or "shell" is called an "exuvia." It is also easy to see the old trachea ligaments protruding from the opening of the cast skin. The false "eye spots" just behind their head on their prothorax help in deterring predators. Their frail bodies are soft and a pale white color. This is called a "teneral" adult. Initially, their wings are crumbled and compacted. After being exposed to the air, the wings slowly unfold and expand as blood is pumped into their veins through more musculature contractions. The wings continue their expansion until they exceed past the tip of their abdomens. These insects look very beautiful during this stage since light reflecting off their bodies remind me of Christmas lights.

Cicada nymph

After taking a short rest, the cicada will eventually sit up and clutch their old shell to remove the rest of their body. Their abdomens are the last to be pulled free. The whole process can take as little as 20 minutes or over an hour depending upon conditions and/or environmental factors. This "teneral" stage will last for days. It may be several hours before their bodies darken and several more days before they will be able to fly.

Their exuviae, sometimes referred to as "ghosts," can remain on trees and branches for many months long after the adult has died. One can differentiate the sexes of each exuvia by examining the ventral side near the tip of the abdomens. The last exterior segment will be phallic and tapered if it's a male. If it's a female, the extremity will have a vaginal contour.

Cicadas emerging in large numbers will often overcrowd themselves and compete for available space. The nymphs will tumble and climb over one another and can dislodge their other brothers and sisters from the side of the tree. Cicadas that have freshly molted and have tumbled from a considerable height will often perish from their fall. Others may become crippled since their wings will no longer fully expand. Cicadas will even try molting on top of other cicadas who are already trying to remove themselves from their own nymphal skins. These less fortunate cicadas may become trapped inside their shells since the other cicada clinging to the top of them will restrict their movements.

Either from temperature fluctuation or inadequate moisture levels, more cicadas may not successfully molt and become trapped and/or only partially free of their old skins. These cicadas will eventually die, either baked by the sun or eaten by scavengers. During a dense emergence, it is not uncommon to find piles of exuviae or dying adults lying on the ground. Those adult cicadas with the deformed or shriveled wings found near the foot of the trees are more susceptible to predation. Some of these adults, now in their final "imago," stage, still manage to lead successful lives despite their handicaps.

It is estimated that approximately 30 percent will die during the ecdysis process due to interrupted or failed molting.

Large emergences occur over a couple of weeks with peak numbers consisting of just a few nights is fascinating to witness. With each new night, fresh nymphs emerge from the ground and begin their ascent into the trees. The arrival of these newcomers will often force the older exuviae and trapped adults from their perches to make room for their latest round of ecdysis.

PERIODICAL CICADA ECDYSIS

A Magicicada nymph climbs the side of a tree where it firmly secures itself

Muscle contractions begin as the exoskeleton splits open down the mesothorax

The opening widens as the nymph continues its muscular contractions to free itself

The head is freed followed by its torso and legs

The cicada leans back to rest. The trachea is clearly visible protruding from the exuvia

After taking a short rest, the cicada will eventually sit up and clutch their old shell to remove the rest of their body. Their abdomens are the last to be pulled free. The whole process can take as little as 20 minutes or over an hour depending upon conditions and/or environmental factors. This "teneral" stage will last for days. It may be several hours before their bodies darken and several more days before they will be able to fly.

After a short rest, the cicada sits up and clutches its exuvia. The cicada then pulls its abdomen free as its wings have already begun to expand

While clinging to a sturdy support, the cicada pumps blood into its wing veins. The wings slowly expand until they extend beyond the abdomen

The wings harden and fold roof-like over the cicada's back

Within a few hours, the cicada's body will harden and become darker

Teneral adult & exuvia

Teneral adult

It will be a few days before the cicada's body will be completely hardened allowing the insect to sing and fly. This is called a teneral adult

Their exuviae sometimes referred to as "ghosts," can remain on trees and branches for many months long after the adult has died. One can differentiate the sexes of each exuvia by examining the ventral side near the tip of the abdomens. The last exterior segment will be phallic and tapered if it's a male. If it's a female, the extremity will have a vaginal contour.

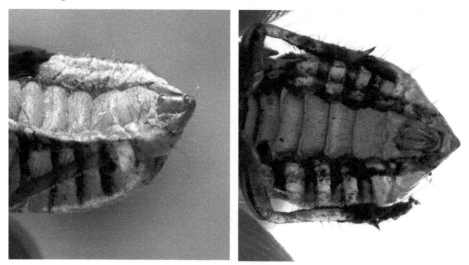

Exuvia gender comparison (Male: Left) (Female: Right)

Periodical cicada exuvia

Periodical cicada exuvia

Cicadas emerging in large numbers will often overcrowd themselves and compete for available space.

Adult cicada & exuvia

Teneral adult & nymph

Various images of periodical cicada ecdysis

The nymphs will tumble and climb over one another and can dislodge their other brothers and sisters from the side of the tree. Cicadas that have freshly molted and have tumbled from a considerable height will often perish from their fall. Others may become crippled since their wings will no longer fully expand. Cicadas will even try molting on top of other cicadas who are already trying to remove themselves from their own nymphal skins. These less fortunate cicadas may become trapped inside their shells since the other cicada clinging to the top of them will restrict their movements.

Periodical cicadas competing for available space during ecdysis

Either from temperature fluctuation or inadequate moisture levels, more cicadas may not successfully molt and become trapped and/or only partially free of their old skins. These cicadas will eventually die, either baked by the sun or eaten by scavengers. During a dense emergence, it is not uncommon to find piles of exuviae or dying adults lying on the ground. Those adult cicadas with the deformed or shriveled wings found near the foot of the trees are more susceptible to predation. Some of these adults, now in their final "imago," stage, still manage to lead successful lives despite their handicaps.

Crippled adults

Faulty ecdysis

Adults trapped within their exuvia

Helpless adults under siege by marauding ants

It is estimated that approximately 30 percent will die during the ecdysis process due to interrupted or failed molting.

Large emergences occur over a couple of weeks with peak numbers consisting of just a few nights is fascinating to witness. With each new night, fresh nymphs emerge from the ground and begin their ascent into the trees. The arrival of these newcomers will often force the older exuviae and trapped adults from their perches to make room for their latest round of ecdysis.

Discarded exuviae

Teneral adults

Adult cicada & exuvia

THE "IMAGO" OR ADULT PERIODICAL CICADA

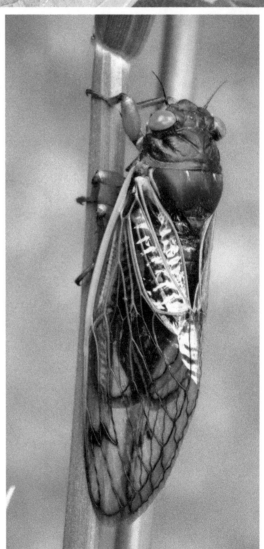

"Cassin's and/or dwarf periodical cicada" Magicicada cassini

"Linnaeus' 17 year cicada" Magicicada septendecim

COURTSHIP and COPULATION

Several days after emerging, male cicadas will begin their singing to attract mates. Male cicadas produce their loud song with the assistance of vibrating ribbed membranes called "tymbals." These organs are located on the underside of their hollow abdomens just behind their hind legs. The cicada sings by rapidly contracting their internal tymbal muscles, causing the membranes to buckle inward before relaxing back to their normal position. This rapid succession produces their distinctive species songs. If you carefully open a male's wings, you'll clearly see these exposed membranes that look like an eardrum. Only male cicadas have these pellicles that produce sound. Female cicadas have no audible organs and remain silent throughout their lives.

The sound the male cicada produces is the loudest in the insect world and can be heard up to a 1/4 mile away. Singing usually commences during the early morning hours and will continue throughout the day until dusk. Different species prefer to sing at different times. Listen carefully and you'll be able to tell the difference in their songs. The song of Magicicada (tredecim) septendecim is the loud "Pharaoh" or "Phar-aoh" sound. You can hear them calling out the ancient Egyptian King if one suspends their belief. Magicicada (tredecassini) cassini's song is a series of clicks followed by a loud

Sound producing organ "tymbal" exposed

"zip," while Magicicada (tredecula) septendecula resembles the noise of a lawn sprinkler.

Unlike certain species of annual cicada, hybridization is rare among periodical cicadas since their females are usually non-responsive to the calls from other species not her own.

Cicadas stop singing once it becomes dark and it is believed the insects are light sensitive where sunlight triggers them to begin trilling again. Male cicadas can gather and produce mass singing aggregations called "chorusing centers." They produce a sound so loud that it's nearly impossible to carry on a conversation or let alone think. The chorus makes it hard for an animal, such as a bird, to pinpoint an exact location of their source since the sound carries far and wide. The intense volume of the chorus may also deter predators that are simply unfamiliar to it, especially since these cicadas remain unseen for many years. An annual cicada is actually louder than a periodical cicada if measured by individual insect. But due to the periodical cicada's abundance, it's their combined might that make their calls deafening.

Mating and offspring success are greater in areas with higher densities. Large aggregations of singing males actually assist the cicada in mate selection. A female cicada is drawn to the sound and has a preference in selecting the largest male of the group. This is common among most species in nature. Females will flick their wings in response to the calls indicating her interest and to catch the attention of a prospecting suitor. A conspecific male responds to the receptive wing clicking by dropping out of the chorus to start courtship advances. The male may fly to her general location if she is farther away. Once in proximity, he will "call walk" towards her by singing and then walking in her direction before stopping to sing again. He may repeat this over and over while she continues her communication with wing flicks. The male must act with haste otherwise another receptive male may try to intrude upon their courtship ritual.

Once the male is chosen, he will produce a different mating sound which is reminisce of an excited person and also signals his intent! The two of them will inosculate at the abdomen and will remain conjoined for several hours. When the female is "sexually satisfied" after receiving his sperm, she will begin to withdraw from the male in order to free herself. I've observed the male get the worst end of this (no humor intended) as he is often dragged about until they are separated. This sexual "tug of war" can cause the mating pair to drop from the trees where they are easily stepped on or eaten by predators. It is believed female cicadas will probably mate only once since they receive a copulatory or vaginal "plug" from her partner that will prevent her from mating again. The male on the other hand may mate several more times.

Magicicada cassini copulation

Magicicada septendecim copulation

MORTALITY & PREDATOR SATIATION

Each species have their own way in dealing with predators. Annual cicadas are very alert and will fly off quickly when approached with danger. Periodical cicadas take a different approach. Due to their extreme magnitude, periodical cicadas suffer from what zoologists call "predator foolhardiness." This means the cicadas will look danger in the face and will make little or no attempt to avert it. Hence, many will be eaten and/or destroyed.

Mole tracks

When the cicadas first appear en masse, predators such as birds, snakes, squirrels, raccoons, skunks, livestock, and even domestic pets, will gorge on them and simply become too full to consume any more. During these emergence years, predators will actually flourish better. Moles become very active prior to an emergence and tend to disrupt lawns.

As they continue emerging in larger numbers wave after wave, the predator attacks decrease. By the second or third week when cicadas begin to procreate, they can do so without being disturbed. When a biotic community is so plentiful that their enemies cannot possibly ravage them all is called "predator satiation." But as their numbers begin to decline in late June and early July, predators once again become a factor in eliminating the remaining few.

Cicadas normally live only a few weeks. They appear in the middle of May (Mid-April for more Southern broods) and will be gone by mid-July in time for a second round of annual cicadas. Once the cicadas begin dying off, their decaying bodies litter the ground and accumulate in dense piles that bake in the hot summer sun. These sun roasted corpses emit repugnant odors that can be easily recognized several yards away.

Deceased adults

Expired female

Female cicadas will die upon completion of laying their eggs. I've located female cicadas that had expired with their ovipositors still lodged in the wood of a twig. Once they die, cicadas drop to the earth where their bodies are dismembered by ants and other scavengers.

Aside from eluding predators, many cicadas will suffer from a fungal infection called "Massospora cicadina." This fungus lays dormant on the surface of the ground for 13 or 17 years and will affect the emerging cicadas that come forth during their brood years. This fungus attacks the Magicicadas exclusively and will grow inside the cicada's abdomen until it breaks open and falls off. Once the abdomen is disjoined, the chalky white fungal spores will be released back onto the ground. There they will remain dormant and affect the offspring of the next cicada generation many years down the road. This fungus renders the cicada incapable of reproducing and will eventually kill it. However, cicadas instilled with the fungus will continue their mating efforts and further spread the infection throughout the cicada community. The fungus has little effect on the overall numbers of the cicada population and is the only organism the cicada's long life span cannot escape.

Ants scavenging cicada corpse

Massospora cicadina

Victim of Massospora cicadina

Cicada killer

Besides birds and fungal infections, another chief cicada predator is the female cicada killer wasp (Specius speciosus). The wasp hunts cicadas primarily by sight and sound. These wasps appear in July and target annual cicadas since by that time; most periodical cicadas will already be gone. Once the wasp locates a cicada, she tackles it and stings it. The sting merely paralyzes the cicada and renders it helpless. The sting also acts as a natural preserving agent and will keep the cicada's body from deteriorating. Her larvae hatch in an underground burrow she stocks with the living cicada. There, the poor cicada will be slowly drained of its bodily fluids while it is still alive! Reminds you of a horror movie, right? More on this vampire-style tale can be found in a later chapter.

Another main factor in controlling the cicada populous is severe weather conditions. Heavy rains and strong winds will often dislodge cicadas from the trees causing them to drop to the ground and drown. I have seen hapless cicadas tumbling and climbing over one another to escape flooding waters.

It has been estimated that approximately 40 percent of all cicada populations will perish from predator attacks, another 40 percent will die from thunderstorms and inclement weather, while the remaining 20 percent insure the survival of the next generation. There have been instances where isolated broods were possibly eradicated by extreme weather. These meteorological conditions were believed to have reduced their adult numbers so drastically that there wasn't enough of their surviving offspring to satiate their predators. As the weeks go by, the adults die and their bodies drop to the ground or near the foot of the trees. Their decay will benefit the plant life since their bodies are full of nitrogen and other nutrients that become natural fertilizer for the soil.

Cicadas during a storm

Deceased female cicada

CICADA DEFENSES

Cicadas have no stingers, chemical weapons, or odors that will deter predators and no actual methods of self-defense. They are herbivores that are often easily picked off by hungry predators but will sometimes drop to the ground when trying to avoid the approach of enemies. Male cicadas give off an audible alarm call or loud "squawk" when attacked by a predator. This sound is very powerful and in combination of the intense vibration originating from the cicada's body, the predator may be startled and drop it. As stated earlier, cicada songs are carried over a great distance and when done in conjunction with other singing males, will often confuse a predator and make it near impossible for them to locate the individual insect. When sound levels increase to these alarming rates, it can actually frighten their enemies.

However, a new mystery and studies have begun in recent years involving the relationships between birds and periodical cicadas. Months prior to a large emergence, there is a decline in the number of many bird species such as blue jays and crows. It is theorized the amplified volume of millions of cicadas drown out the communication within these bird species and are forcing them to fly to other locations. The birds may deprive themselves of a healthy food source but how do they know what years the cicadas are set to emerge and what causes their decline before the insects actually appear? Plant growth tends to slow in years prior to an emergence, so perhaps there is some unknown biological mechanism that helps the cicadas in repelling predators? Once a brood year is finished, the bird populations increase significantly before returning to normal levels.

Cicadas have a long beak called a "rostrum" tucked between their front legs they use for piercing twigs to draw nourishment and to retain moisture. People have reported to have been allegedly "stung" by the cicada. In all of the years I've handled cicadas, I can recall twice where a cicada tried to insert its beak into my finger after apparently mistaking it for a twig. The puncture reminded me of a pin prick and I felt no real pain. Once the cicadas realized their mistake, they quickly withdrew and didn't make a second attempt. The so-called cicada "bite" left no mark or swelling.

ADULT FEEDING HABITS

It was once believed adult cicadas didn't feed at all. From my observations during the humid weeks of late June, I recall seeing many adult cicadas clustered in groups to the side of several small trees. They were feeding on the sap or "xylem" and reminded me of animals gathered at a watering hole. The cicadas had their beak-like mouth-parts or "rostrums" buried deeply into the surface of the wood. Occasionally, these adults would excrete waste called "honeydew" from the pours of their abdomens whose fluids resembled tiny droplets of rain falling to the ground. When large groups of cicadas feed together in a tree canopy, they can create what appears to be artificial precipitation.

I've seen ants scurrying around and harassing these undaunted feeding cicadas. The ants were attempting to seize a quick drink from the hollows in the bark the cicadas had created. If an ant began to irritate a drinking cicada, the cicada would merely swat at the nuisance with its front legs or flick its wings in protest. These actions usually deter the ants into bothering some other individual. I've also observed small wasps and flies agitating feeding cicadas with enough persistence that the cicada eventually abandoned its drinking hole and flew away.

So how do cicadas eat? Their rostrums contain muscles in what appears to be a cicada's nose which siphons the xylem the same way one uses a straw to drink a beverage. The needle-like outer part is called the labium which contains a stylet. The stylet also consists of two parts called the mandibles and maxillae which work together to penetrate and draw the nutrients from the plant. Much like mosquitoes, cicadas will inject the plant with saliva that actually seals any hole their feeding may have caused. Once the fluid is inside the cicada's body, bacterial components assist in digesting and breaking down the amino acids so that the energy can be suitably processed.

Feeding cicadas

EGGS & OVIPOSITING

Cicadas begin laying eggs or "ovipositing" at approximately 10 days after their initial emergence and persists in doing so into early July or until all of them are gone. The eggs are deposited mostly during the peak temperatures of the afternoon when they are the most active.

Cicadas will deposit between 400 to 600 eggs that resemble grains of rice. The eggs are laid in live branches about the width of a pencil that a female can easily grasp between her legs. Different species of cicadas choose different sizes of branches that are in conjunction to their overall body mass. This helps in preventing twig breakage and nest overlapping among the distinct species.

Cicada eggs protruding from the corpse of a deceased female

Magicicada cassini ovipositing

Magicicada septendecim ovipositing

The eggs are laid just under the surface of the branch in V-shaped chambers. These wooden chambers are carved out by the female cicada's egg laying instrument called an "ovipositor." This organ is kept hidden in a sheath located on the underside of her abdomen until ready for use. The ovipositor is shaped like a spear and has serrated edges that perform a function like a saw in excavating these compartments. The nests may contain as many as 5 to 30 eggs. Their numbers vary among each species as does the distinctive shape of the nests themselves.

Close up of ovipositor inserted into branch

Magicicada septendecim ovipositing

Female removing ovipositor from branch

The individual nests are dug out of the wood at approximate 45 degree angles that curve inward from their openings. The mother cicada is careful not to thrust too hard in order to avoid punching through the opposite side of the branch.

Each of the eggs is placed side by side in an orderly single file. The female thrusts her ovipositor deep into the opening each time she deposits an egg before retracting it. She repeats this motion to make another deposit in an accompanying roll of eggs alongside the first. The whole process may take at least fifteen minutes to complete a single nest before she moves slightly up the branch to begin another.

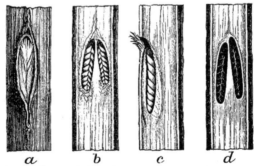

FIG. 33.—Egg nest of the Cicada: *a*, recent puncture, front view; *b*, same, surface removed to show arrangement of eggs, from above; *c*, same, side view; *d*, egg cavity exposed after eggs are removed, and showing the sculpture left by the ovipositor—all enlarged (after Riley).

Drawing of cicada egg nests

(Source: Marlatt, C.L. 1907. The periodical cicada. U.S.D.A. Bur. Entomol. Bull.)

Egg nests & scars

If left undisturbed, she will likely make up to dozen or more nests in a single branch or as many as fifty, thus leaving a long line of puncture holes and frayed wood in her wake. Multiple females performing this task on the same limb will take its toll on the branch's overall integrity, causing it to splinter and scar.

Nest punctures holes

Ovipositing female M. septendecim

These repetitive methods can often kill branches but are natural pruning processes that help eliminate the weaker offshoots. The drooping vegetation that results is commonly referred to as "flagging" since the wilted limbs snap easily when touched and resemble "flags" flapping in the wind. It is not uncommon to find these broken branches scattered across the forest floor after a storm. The eggs swell as they collect nutrients from the plant's living tissue but many perish if the branches they inhabit break off prematurely during the early weeks of their development. The dead eggs may change color to a yellow, brown, or red.

Flagging damage

Broken limbs after a storm due to flagging

If an ovipositing female is disturbed by another cicada, she merely swats at them with her front legs. This is often enough to give the intruding cicada a subtle hint. The trespassing cicada will either walk or fly away to another branch.

During a heavy cicada emergence, the damage done by ovipositing is very apparent and many trees will have brown withered leaves from top to bottom. Many saplings, younger trees, and bushes are often used since they usually live and insure the survival of their offspring over the next 17 years. Unfortunately, some of the younger plants die from this mass egg laying onslaught. Cicadas can be serious pests to ornamental trees and orchards since their habits slow plant productivity and fruit yield.

Young trees severely damaged due to excessive ovipositing

Trees suffering flagging damage

Cicadas prefer deciduous forest trees such as ash, oak, hickory, maple, elm, birch, apple, peach, pear, dogwood, hawthorn, walnut, magnolia, willow, cypress, sycamore and many other species of trees and/or plants. I've also seen thorn bushes used by the species, Magicicada cassini. Magicicada septendecula has a preference for walnuts and hickories.

Cicadas will oviposit in pine but those trees are not a favorable host. Their hatch rate is significantly reduced when oviposited in conifers due to the tree's sticky resin that can encase and trap the eggs within their nests. If hatching is successful, nymphs have no issues feeding upon the coniferous roots. Eggs can also become trapped inside their chambers of deciduous trees if the tree heals over its wounds at the nest opening.

Cicada eggs are very vulnerable to predators such as mites and certain species of parasitic flies which

*Ovipositing female Magicicada septendecim
with an unwelcomed visitor*

lay their eggs near that of the cicadas.' The fly eggs hatch before the cicada eggs and the larvae will make a meal of the cicada's unborn family.

Asides from insect parasites, oviposition punctures can remain open for several years thus allowing other insect species to take up temporary residency in these vacant roosts.

Female cicadas will oviposit away from chorusing centers. They prefer forest edges and clearings since they are better maintained as opposed to the congested forest. Female cicadas choose trees with healthier crowns and those that have more exposure to light. Another preference is along wooded waterways where the land isn't disturbed by agriculture. Perhaps the reason for these preferences are due to the proximity of lower nearby vegetation, like grasses, in which newly hatched nymphs feed upon the first year of their lives. Also, new tree roots grow faster and denser along forest edges with more open terrain. Cicadas that emerge from these areas are found to be bigger and healthier than those that emerge in the heavier forested environments.

Ovipositing female

Cicadas don't migrate and don't normally stray far from their original birth site. Habitation disturbances sometimes force cicadas to choose secondary growth vegetation and in doing so, thrive well upon it. Since habitats change over 17 years, cicadas are affected by this and reposition their offspring accordingly. Nymphs are known to emerge from the ground even after their host tree has been long since cut down.

THE NEWBORN NYMPHS

If all goes well, the eggs hatch between six and eight weeks. After about two weeks, the red eye spots become visible underneath the egg shell. When ready, the newborn cicada nymphs hatch out of their egg casing that has become soft like a skin membrane, leaving the discarded shells behind. Nymphs are covered in a protective embryotic epidermis that keeps their legs and antennae pressed against their frail bodies. The nymphs wiggle toward the nest opening where they dangle at the entrance while remaining secured by their embryonic sleeves. The nymphs free themselves by discarding this skin where they begin scurrying about the branch.

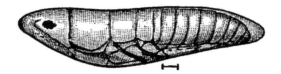

Drawing of unhatched egg

(Source: Marlatt, C.L. 1907. The periodical cicada. U.S.D.A. Bur. Entomol. Bull.)

The nymphs are blind and ant-like in appearance, with small hairs on their bodies. The "fossorial" forelegs of the nymphs are enlarged and designed for digging and grasping dirt. They are approximately one sixteenth of an inch in length and lighter than air. They will either leap or the first gentle breeze will dislodge them and cause them to fall gently to the turf.

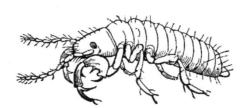

Drawing of newly hatched 1st instar nymph

(Source: Marlatt, C.L. 1907. The periodical cicada. U.S.D.A. Bur. Entomol. Bull.)

Once on the ground, the nymphs again must scurry about until they come across the first crevice or other opening. If that first crack or crevice doesn't yield a rootlet, the nymphs will return to the surface and seek another. They will then descend into the dark depths of the earth and remain there for the next 13 or 17 years, depending upon the species. The nymphs must hurry since they are very vulnerable to predation by ants, mites, spiders, and other enemies. Also, the hot sun will eventually kill them if they fail to make haste.

There have been reports of increased oak mite activity coinciding with the cicada hatches in oak trees. Oak mites are known to attack the larvae of other insects but tend to drop down on unsuspecting humans and leave behind itchy welts.

THE SUBTERRANEAN EXISTENCE

Once the nymphs begin their descent into the soil, they will feed on the fluids of grasses for the first year. Afterward they will dig deeper into the earth to a depth between two to eighteen inches in search of a suitable tree root to draw their nourishment. Nymphs have also been found at depths greater than two feet.

After a rootlet is established, a nymph doesn't relocate more than just a few inches during the rest of its long underground life. Nymphs will construct a cell up to 5 times the length of their bodies using their own secretions. The cell walls will be impermeable and protect them from drowning during heavy rains and flooding conditions.

Not all periodical cicadas are concerned with flood waters. Magicicada cassini are a lowland species. They prosper in flood plain areas where portions of the land they dwell can be submerged underwater for long periods of time. Their cousins, Magicicada septendecim and Magicicada septendecula, are the opposite and prefer to inhabit higher elevations.

The nymphs grow very slowly and will be safe from a lot of enemies. Even underground, moles, beetle larvae, ants, and other ground dwelling predators can encounter the nymphs and devour many of them. Nymphs also suffer mortality from failing to locate suitable host rootlets and from parasitic fungi. Very little is known about the nymph's underground life for it is very hard to study. It is estimated that up to 98 percent of the nymphs won't survive beyond the first 2 years of their lives.

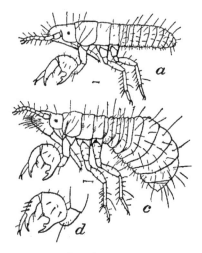

Drawing of underground nymphs

(Source: Marlatt, C.L. 1907. The periodical cicada. U.S.D.A. Bur. Entomol. Bull.)

The cicada nymphs undergo five growth stages or "instars" during their subterranean existence. Upon completion of each instar stage, the nymphs will shed their old skin in order to grow larger. Their cells will also be enlarged to accommodate their growth or they will relocate in search of a larger root. The first instar stage for the 17 year species lasts for approximately 1 year, the second instar is approximately 2 years, the third is up to 4 years, the fourth is another 3 to 4, and the fifth is between 6 to 8 years. Nymphal maturity or fifth instar is generally reached between nine and twelve years.

13-year cicadas develop at similar times but spend 3 to 4 years in their last instar. The 17-year species grow slower, especially in their first few years. Whether they are a 13 or 17 year cicada, not all nymphs mature at the same rate and some will take longer or shorter to reach full nymphal maturity. The reason may be in part due to limited or inadequate food sources or from overcrowded conditions and species competition. The species, M. septendecula are believed to retard their development by a year because of species competition in mixed populations.

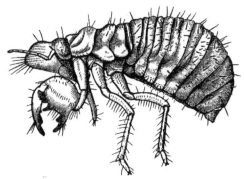

Drawing of 4th instar nymph

(Source: Marlatt, C.L. 1907. The periodical cicada. U.S.D.A. Bur. Entomol. Bull.)

These conditions can sometimes force off schedule emergences. Nymphs that emerge too early or too late from the rest of their brood are known as "stragglers." Sometimes "straggling" can be 1 to 4 years early or 1 or more years late. 18 year stragglers are usually not numerous enough to produce a significant amount of offspring that can survive past the next generation. Those emerging 4 years early in somewhat larger numbers have been observed reproducing with some success and only time will tell if their offspring will be the evolution of a new brood. Such instances have been recorded in Southern Ohio over the past couple of decades.

During the winter months, the nymphs will become dormant and survive a long duration without food.

After they achieve their maximum size and if all goes as nature has originally intended, they will climb upward and wait between 4 and 8 inches underground until their 13th or 17th year. Waiting until that strange unknown phenomenon once again summons them from the earth. Up until then, they will live below the surface in the desolate corridors they make for themselves, alone in the darkness and in complete isolation they call their home.

VI
AN ACCOUNT SUMMARY
FOR BROOD V: 1999

LOCATION: Findley State Park, located 3 miles south of Wellington, Lorain County, Ohio.

MONDAY, MAY 17th: The first individuals are seen emerging from the ground.

WEDNESDAY, MAY 19th: A light emergence is observed with M. septendecim being the only species located.

FRIDAY, MAY 21st: The emergence is growing heavier with individuals emerging as late as 0700 to 1000 hours. Only M. septendecim is seen and some faint singing is heard. Additional emerging isn't observed again until 1930 hours where numerous nymphs are easily spotted crawling across the ground and heard trampling through the leaf litter on the forest floor. By 2030 hours, the ground appears to be alive with crawling nymphs. This emergence continues way into the night.

Nymphs crawling along the ground

Cicada nymph

SUNDAY, MAY 23rd: Many more nymphs continue to emerge. The first M. cassini and M. decula have also begun to appear and are located between camp sites 95 through 99. The first indications of fungal infection are found in a few adults.

WEDNESDAY, MAY 26th: Cold damp day. Singing is heard with fresh teneral adults covering both tree trunks and branches from a heavy overnight emergence. Exit holes perforate the ground and exuviae decorate the trunks of nearly every tree. Dead and dying adults clutter the ground after being victims of faulty molts and overcrowded conditions. Birds are observed feeding on live adults with a few fluttering to the ground to evade them. The emergence of all species continues through the morning hours.

Teneral adult & exuvia

THURSDAY, MAY 27th: Singing is heard with increased volume and increased population. More nymphs appear after 1900 hours in extraordinary numbers.

FRIDAY, MAY 28th: Warm day, approximately 75-80 degrees Fahrenheit. Their singing becomes loud and constant. During the hours of 1900 to 2100, another large emergence of nymphs comes forth from the ground. They are so abundant that they are actually climbing over one another in a race to reach the nearest tree. Many actually try climbing the legs of my tripod and one individual made it up my pant leg to my knee!

SATURDAY, MAY 29th: Another warm day with increased singing and volume. Many more emerging nymphs and teneral adults are seen during the early morning hours. Honeydew occasionally falls from the trees above like short periods of rain. The first odor of decay from the dying adults is detected with help from the baking sun. The number of living adults is incredible as the entire park has become inundated with them!

Magicicada septendecim

TUESDAY, JUNE 1st: Light overnight emergence. Singing is loud and non-stop. A few adults are found deceased after having drowned from rain the previous day. Fungal infections are increasingly noticeable.

WEDNESDAY, JUNE 2nd: Rain sweeps across much of Northern Ohio.

FRIDAY, JUNE 4th: Warm day with pleasant weather. Nymphs are still emerging but in fewer numbers. Fungal infections have spread throughout the population. More dead litter the ground and emit odors of decay. Adults are clinging to just about everything and are very active. Approximately a dozen pairs of mating adults are observed sitting on/or close to the ground. The first ovipositing females are spotted on low hanging branches. Singing is extremely loud and deafening at the peak of the day as millions of males form chorusing centers in the surrounding trees.

Magicicada septendecim

Magicicada septendecim copulating

SUNDAY, JUNE 6th: Hot, 90 degree day. The singing is again extremely loud while mating and ovipositing have become a widespread frenzy throughout the park. The mating urge has become so powerful that one male was seen trying to mount a dead female whose corpse was still hanging on a limb.

TUESDAY, JUNE 8th: Another hot, 90 degree day. The song volume is excessive. No ovipositing is observed during the morning hours and appears to resume later in the afternoon. The fungal infection continues to spread along with the increased number of dead and dying. The odor of death is strong with the summer heat. Emerging appears to have ceased altogether.

Fungal infection Massospora cicadina

FRIDAY, JUNE 11th: The chorus volume is piercing and unrelenting while mating and ovipositing is omni-present. Honeydew falls during the height of another hot day. The decaying odors are repugnant as the dead and dying are occasionally found dropping from the upper branches.

Magicicada septendecim ovipositing

MONDAY, JUNE 21st: Warm, 80 degree day. The choruses of all three species are heard. The sound is strong but slightly decreased. The fungal infections continue to spread while mating and ovipositing have become the driving force of their existence. The first and only cross breeding pair is observed between a male cassini and a female septendecim. Piles of the dead and dying adults are accumulating. Flagging damage is apparent on a myriad of trees. Their leaves are found withered and their branches are easily broken if bumped. The damage is even more evident on younger saplings. Some branches bleed sap from the wounds sustained from ovipositing. Egg damage is also found on small thorn bushes.

Flagging

MONDAY, JUNE 28th: The chorus has greatly diminished as is the number of live adults. Females are still ovipositing and younger trees have suffered much flagging damage. Fungal infected adults are clustered on lower limbs and grasses. One male cassini is observed trying to mount a septendecim missing an abdomen. Carcasses litter the trails and roadways. The dying appears to be more female than male while their decaying odors remain overwhelming. Their corpses are consumed by ants and fly maggots while others simply bake in the hot sun. The first annual cicadas songs are heard between approximately 3 to 4 males and a half dozen of their exuviae are found clung to some small trees.

TUESDAY, JUNE 29th: A cool, damp 60 degree morning caused by a low pressure system the night before. Many more dead have fallen from the trees, evidently more female than male. Dead branches from excessive flagging are scattered across the ground. Very few living adults are seen with many of those infected by the fungus. The once loud chorusing has been reduced to mere fragmented calls. The number of annual cicada exuviae is on the rise.

Deceased adults & exuviae

THURSDAY, JULY 8th: A handful of living adults are left, mostly female. The faint calls from a few cassini and a solitary decula and septendecim are heard briefly. The piles of lifeless cicadas are everywhere and their stench is powerful. The remaining living adults are moribund and too tired to avoid both detection and/or predation. One female is observed trying to lay eggs but is too feeble to insert her ovipositor into the bark. Another female is found recently expired with her ovipositor inserted into a twig containing her final nest. The younger trees have suffered severe flagging damage with some appearing to be completely dead. More damaged and scarred branches lay splintered on the forest floor. Annual cicadas emit their calls intermittently.

FRIDAY, JULY 9th: Severe thunderstorms with heavy rains and high winds hit much of Northern Ohio.

SUNDAY, JULY 11th: Cool day. No living adults are seen or heard. The evidence of decay and broken limbs remain piled at the foot of the trees. There are so many trees that weep with flagging damage; I would have blamed the weather had I not witnessed the underlying cause over the past month. The annuals are the only cicadas left singing whose songs are gaining strength. The Brood V saga has ended for Findley State Park.

AN ACCOUNT SUMMARY FOR BROOD V: 2016 - 17 YEARS LATER

LOCATION: Findley State Park, located 3 miles south of Wellington, Lorain County, Ohio.

MONDAY, MAY 23rd: The emergence has finally begun at the Findley State Park after a prolonged cold spring. The first wave is light and spotty throughout the park but there is a fair amount of cast skins, ecdysis in progress, nymphs moving about, and teneral adults of M. septendecim. There appears to be a lot more males than females at this time. There are also plenty of mud chimneys and exit holes, especially under coniferous tree canopies. The overnight low for the area was approximately 42 degrees Fahrenheit but climbed to 76 degrees by the early afternoon.

Cicada chimneys

TUESDAY, MAY 24th: Another light spotty emergence where I observed birds preying on cicadas near the picnic areas. When I arrived today at 0900 hours, the temperature was approximately 67 degrees and climbed to 79 degrees by 1300 hours.

WEDNESDAY, MAY 25th: Heavier overnight emergence on this date and now throughout the entire park. I'm seeing an equal amount of females to males. "Honeydew" pelts me while inspecting the trees. A warm front has increased the daily temperatures. By 0820 hours, temperatures were approximately 69 degrees and increased to 81 degrees by 1120.

FRIDAY, MAY 27th: A larger emergence overnight has plenteous exuviae covering the trunks and branches of many trees with emerging nymphs and teneral adults occupying the grasses. The dropping of "honeydew" is more frequent and adults clutter the paved parking areas and drinking fountains. Some have become strong fliers and one male emitted a loud "shriek" when I picked him up. As I stood under the trees, several kept landing on me. I had to keep moving to avoid nymphs scaling up my body after one made it as high as my chest! The first specimens of M. cassini are observed near the park's camp store and there are many individuals with malformed wings. I detect the first odor of decay near trees beside the picnic areas. It is a clear warm day where the temperature was approximately 69 degrees at 0720 hours increasing to 82 degrees by 1230.

Exuvia

Magicicada septendecim

SUNDAY, MAY 29th: Warm partly cloudy day after an evening of storms. The emergence has become heavy as cast skins and teneral adults weigh down the smaller branches. It is near impossible to walk in the grass with the amount of nymphs and adults either wandering or resting there. Piles of discarded exuviae and dead adults from faulty molting lie at the bases of the trees. In addition, it has also become hard to drive on the paved streets without swerving to avoid resting adults. While standing under a tree, I receive a shower of excreted "honeydew" courtesy of a cicada somewhere above. Chorusing has also begun during the morning hours shortly after 0900. The temperature was a mild 73 degrees when I arrived at 0730 hours and only increased to 76 degrees 3 hours later.

Heavy emergence

WEDNESDAY, JUNE 1st: Another warm day but with a cool start. At 0730 hours, the temperature was 63 degrees but rose to 77 by 1030. The emergence was heavy over the last several days. The piles of discarded exuviae and crippled adults have escalated and are smothering the vegetation. Some individuals even made it inside the public restrooms. The chorusing had already started on my arrival where I detected all 3 species. Their volume increased with the rise of the temperature. The Massospora cicadina fungal infection is present in several areas of the park.

Faulty ecdysis

THURSDAY, JUNE 9th: Cool, partly cloudy day. Temperatures during my visit remained in the mid-sixties. Despite the cooler weather, the chorusing centers were strong and ear piercing. Only one new teneral was observed while the piles of the dead emitted more odors of decay. Expired adults are found almost everywhere along with widespread fungal infections. I discover dozens of mating pairs but only a few ovipositing females. I did locate some freshly made nests.

SUNDAY, JUNE 12th: Cool windy morning in the mid-sixties. There were no new emerging adults but chorusing remained consistent and loud. Many branches have been inflicted with scars from nest building and the first signs of flagging damage are observed on smaller trees and saplings.

TUESDAY, JUNE 14th: Cloudy day with temperatures at approximately 63 degrees at 0800 and rising to 70 degrees by 1130. Chorusing remains constant but starting to diminish. The fungal infections are epizootic, while mating and flagging damage continues. The dead are increasing along the walking trails and paved roadways.

Magicicada septendecim copulating

WEDNESDAY, JUNE 22nd: Cloudy day in the low eighties. The choruses and overall population has dwindled. The odor of decaying cicada carcasses is insufferable. Females remain busy ovipositing. Flagging damage is very visible.

Magicicada septendecim ovipositing

SUNDAY, JUNE 26th: Hot hazy day in the nineties. Choruses have become faint with occasional outbursts of M. cassini calls. Carcasses litter the ground and flagging damage is ubiquitous. Live adults are becoming scarce.

SATURDAY, JULY 2nd: Cloudy and mild with temperatures in the low seventies. I only locate a handful of living adults but their dead are everywhere. There are faint, weak choruses deep within the woods during brief intervals of light that occasionally peak through the clouds. Isolated M. cassini calls are heard every so often. Flagging damage is abundant throughout the park. A half dozen annual cicada exuviae are observed but no singing is heard from any annual species on this day.

Magicicada cassini with annual cicada exuvia

Flagging damage

WEDNESDAY, JULY 6th: Partly cloudy hot day in the upper eighties. No living adults are seen and there is no more chorusing. Only a few isolated M. cassini and M. septendecim are heard calling on occasion. Within a week, all of them will be gone. There are countless dead littering the ground, walkways, and under trees. The annual cicadas (N. tibicen tibicen) are singing to take their place as the sounds of summer.

SATURDAY, JULY 9th: Partly cloudy mild day in the seventies. Still no living Magicicadas are seen and their singing has ceased completely. The annual cicadas are filling the void with their own songs. I bid farewell again to the Brood V cicadas of Findley State Park.

VII
BROOD MAPS

The following periodical cicada brood maps are the "approximate" areas each brood is expected to appear. They were mapped out by many scientists, naturalists, and volunteers who took a lot of time, gas, and patience to prepare. I'd like to express my gratitude and appreciation for everyone who participates in these endeavors which makes this data readily available. I too, have participated in these mapping projects in the past and it can be quite grueling in having to endure the hot sun, biting insects, and plant allergies.

Why "approximate" I say? Well, plenty go on every 13 or 17 years where environments change all of the time. How many places have you seen shopping malls or housing complexes now standing where once lush woodlands had been a mere decade before? These broods are under constant threat of economic development and human encroachment all of the time and with an ever increasing human population, these pressures will continue to increase. Please read my "The FUTURE" chapter for more details....

Broods were designated with Roman numerals beginning way back in 1893 with Brood I and so on. The first numerals of I through XVII were designated to the known 17 year broods while XVIII through XXX were designated to the 13 year broods. There are currently 12 existing 17 year broods and 3 existing 13 year Broods. Only one known 17 year brood (Brood XI) has been documented as becoming extinct during the past century and was last seen in 1954. The 13 year brood assigned as XXI is also extinct and hasn't been seen since 1870.

Here is the key for reading the following maps:

BLUE DOTS represent 17 year cicada emergence locations.
RED DOTS represent 13 year cicada emergence locations.
GREEN DOTS represent the location of the extinct 17 year Brood.
PURPLE DOTS represent the location of the extinct 13 year Brood.

Also NOTE: There has been previous documentation of small colonies of Magicicadas existing in Southern Canada (Ontario Province) near the United States border. However, like Broods "XI" and "XXI," they too, have sadly gone extinct.

BROOD I
Aka: "Blue Ridge Brood"

Emergence Years: 1995, 2012, 2029, 2046, 2063...
Locations: TN, VA, WV

BROOD II
Aka: "East Coast Brood"

Emergence Years: 1996, 2013, 2030, 2047, 2064...
Locations: CT, GA, MD, NC, NJ, NY, OK, PA, VA

BROOD III
Aka: "Iowan Brood"

Emergence Years: 1997, 2014, 2031, 2048, 2065...
Locations: IA, IL, MO

BROOD IV
Aka: "Kansan Brood"

Emergence Years: 1998, 2015, 2032, 2049, 2066...
Locations: IA, KS, MO, NE, OK, TX

BROOD V

Emergence Years: 1999, 2016, 2033, 2050, 2067...
Locations: NY, OH, PA, VA, WV

BROOD VI

Emergence Years: 2000, 2017, 2034, 2051, 2068...
Locations: GA, OH?, NC, SC

BROOD VII
Aka: "Onondaga Brood"

Emergence Years: 2001, 2018, 2035, 2052, 2069...
Location: NY

BROOD VIII

Emergence Years: 2002, 2019, 2036, 2053, 2070...
Locations: OH, PA, WV

BROOD IX

Emergence Years: 2003, 2020, 2037, 2054, 2071...
Locations: NC, VA, WV

BROOD X

Aka: "Great Eastern Brood"

Emergence Years: 2004, 2021, 2038, 2055, 2072...
Locations: DC, DE, GA, IL, IN, KY, MD, MI, NC, NJ, NY, OH, PA, TN, VA, WV

BROOD XI

Emergence Years: 1937, 1954
Locations: CT, MA, RI

BROOD XIII
Aka: "Northern Illinois Brood"

Emergence Years: 2007, 2024, 2041, 2058, 2075...
Locations: IA, IL, IN, MI, WI

BROOD XIV

Emergence Years: 2008, 2025, 2042, 2059, 2076...
Locations: GA, IN, KY, MA, MD, NC, NJ, NY, OH, PA, TN, VA, WVA

COMPLETE 17 YEAR CICADA BROOD DISTRIBUTION

BROOD XIX
Aka: "Great Southern Brood"

Emergence Years: 1998, 2011, 2024, 2037, 2050...

Locations: AL, AR, GA, IL, IN, KS, KY, LA, MO, MS, NC, OK, SC, TN, VA

BROOD XXI
Aka: "Floridian Brood"

Emergence Year: 1870
Location: FL

BROOD XXII
Aka: "Baton Rouge Brood"

Emergence Years: 2001, 2014, 2027, 2040, 2053...
Locations: KY, LA, MS, OH

BROOD XXIII
Aka: "Lower Mississippi River Valley Brood"

Emergence Years: 2002, 2015, 2028, 2041, 2054...
Locations: AR, IL, IN, KY, LA, MO, MS, TN

COMPLETE 13 YEAR CICADA BROOD DISTRIBUTION

COMPLETE 13 YEAR & 17 YEAR CICADA BROOD DISTRIBUTION

VIII
THE ANNUAL CICADA

"Lyric cicada" Neotibicen lyricen lyricen

By early July, those areas that were previously overwhelmed with periodical cicadas in the spring get a short break from the insatiable noise. By now; nearly all of them will have vanished as mysteriously as they had initially appeared. The woods have fallen silent and the chirps of song birds can be heard once again. This break from the cicada commotion is only temporary.

The average daily temperatures are on the rise and the relentless sun is harsh. Many plants wither and die from the excessive heat as animals go on the hunt for life sustaining water. Most creatures feel the impact as the dog days of summer have quickly descended upon them.

In the middle of the night, a newly awakened creature emerges from the earth and walks among the perforations left behind by its smaller cousins. This creature is strikingly similar and noticeably larger and bulkier. It too begins its ascent into the trees where it removes its outer skin and becomes a creature of flight. Its eyes are dark and its new body is marked with patterns that help it blend better into its surroundings. Within days, a new sound resonates from the tree canopy as the first annual cicada calls abroad to it make its presence known.

Annual cicada nymph

Annual cicada nymph

Annual cicadas are felt every summer when the intense heat of the day is at its hottest. They come in a variety of sizes and colors and like to inhabit residential areas, city parks, rural countryside, as well as dense woodlands. Most are predominately black in color with markings of green, browns, tans, and teals. Their undersides are white or cream colored with some having a black band centered down their abdomens. Smaller species are the size of a large M. septendecim while others exceed two inches in length. Unlike the colorful periodic cicadas, their colors are drabber and designed for camouflage.

Annual cicada (Male ventral view)

Annual cicada (Female ventral view)

According to folklore, they are symbols of the coming harvest and their appearance predicts the first frost in 6 weeks. If that were the case, summer would come to an abrupt end by the middle of August.

They are known by a variety of names too. Dog-day cicadas, harvest flies, harvest men, jar flies, July flies, dry flies, heat bugs, and locusts are the most common from region to region. Whatever their name, the annual cicadas are the foremost backdrop sounds of the season! Their life cycles are similar to that of the periodical cicada but overall, these creatures are neglected by scholars and understudied.

Annual cicada exuvia

Instead of requiring nearly two decades, it is believed that most species only require a growth period of 2 to 5 years, perhaps longer. Their actual developmental duration is unknown. With their life spans being much shorter and their "broods" overlapping one another, they are seen every summer. Seldom do they become abundant enough to cause a real stir and are considered to have no economic importance. They emerge in far fewer numbers and it is rare to find a tree with over a hundred exuviae. On good years they can number as many as 50 or 60.

In the Eastern states, they begin issuing from the ground around late June. Unlike the periodical cicada that emerged in enormous masses over a frame of roughly two weeks, the emergence periods for annual cicadas are much more staggered and continue for approximately 2 to 2 1/2 months. I've seen them emerging into mid-September even after their overall numbers have diminished for that year.

ANNUAL CICADA ECDYSIS

Upon locating a secure perch, muscle contractions begin by splitting the exoskeleton open down the mesothorax

The head emerges followed by its torso and legs

The cicada pauses to rest as its wings begin to unfold. Note the trachea protruding from the exuvia

After resting, the cicada slowly sits up and pulls its body free from its exuvia

*Still grasping its exuvia, the cicada's wings expand until they extend beyond
the length of its abdomen*

The wings harden and fold over the cicada's back

From mid-July to mid-August, several species have emerged and their numbers are at their heaviest. Like the periodical cicadas, several species will sing together and form loud chorusing ensembles. The peak choruses are heard in the mid-morning and again a couple of hours leading up to the sunset.

Different species sing at different times throughout the day with most seemingly resting briefly during the afternoon. The choruses are a unique mix of buzzing, grinding, and pulsating. A careful listener can become accustomed to their sounds and familiar with each species that produces them. In my neck of the woods, their combined sound can nearly reach the volume of their famous 17 year relatives.

Annual Cicadas have all of the same enemies like those of any other cicada. Annual Cicadas react differently when approached with danger and don't easily fall to "predator foolhardiness." These cicadas are quick to take flight and reverberates their distress when they do. Despite being clumsy fliers, it is not uncommon to hear them careening through the branches of trees.

Birds do at times manage to feast on them and can be brutal in their methods while doing so. I've seen crows carrying male cicadas in their beaks where the bird repeatedly slams the insect to the ground despite its sounds of distress and apparent pain. It normally isn't long before the insect goes silent despite my futile efforts in trying to frighten the bird into dropping its quarry.

One of the main enemies is the infamous cicada killer wasp. Menacing in appearance yet docile in its nature, the wasp vigorously hunts its prey throughout the day. I've seen these creatures in action as they are carrying their victim up the side of a tree with little exertion to itself. They are fast and difficult to capture in photographs prior to returning to their burrows with their prize. I'm careful not to startle them for they will abandon the paralyzed cicada and not return for it, making its eventual death

Cicada killer (male)

in vain. More on the cicada "hawk" will be thoroughly discussed in the coming chapter.

Another predator worthy of mention is the cedar beetle or cicada parasite beetle (Sandalus niger). They are black or brown in color, about an inch in length, and appear in September and October. These beetles have a short adult life span, do not eat, and converge in mating clusters before laying eggs in the bark of trees near cicada oviposition sites. The beetle larvae hatch and drop to the ground where they bore in search of cicada nymphs. They attach themselves to the nymphs and become sedentary feeders or ectoparasites by collecting nutrients from the cicada's bodily fluids. The cicada nymph continues to feed but its growth is slowed to where it eventually dies. The larva then pupates and emerges the following summer.

Despite the intense humidity, the annual cicadas continue their serenades while drawing nourishment from the stems they rest upon. Most inhabit the highest parts of sturdy older trees and position themselves on the gnarled wood, making their visibility almost undetectable at times.

Annual cicada feeding

But not all species are found far from the ground. One of the most popular and my personal favorite is the species, Neotibicen tibicen tibicen (formerly known as Tibicen tibicen and Tibicen chloromera) or the "swamp cicada." This insect is predominantly black with a green prothorax and wing views, dark eyes, (that can also be green) and has a powder white ventral side. They are commonly found on lower and often dense vegetation as well as high among the treetops. Their loud morning buzzing sounds are rapid and heard primarily during the hours before noon. They will form loud choruses with other species of cicadas that will turn an otherwise peaceful morning into a loud frenzy of songs. This species is probably the most encountered and is also called the "morning cicada."

The identification of some annual cicada species can be very difficult and frustrating. They can be morphologically and genetically similar and have color variations. Many are very close in size and appearance and a few even have similar calling songs. When the geographical territories of these species overlap, they can create what is known as a hybrid zone. Hybridization among periodical cicadas is rare yet possible. It is more common in the annual species that are described and categorized among the "green" types. In my area of Northwest Ohio, there are several of these generalized "green" types of cicadas such as N. pruinosus pruinosus, the "scissors-grinder," N. linnei, "Linne's Cicada" and N. canicularis.

"The swamp cicada" Neotibicen tibicen tibicen

"Green" species of annual cicadas

The scissors-grinder, N. pruinosus pruinosus, is dusk singers whose rapidly pulsating rhythms slow to a halt are the cue for katydids to begin singing once the daylight disappears. Only once did I ever hear an annual cicada singing in the darkness at approximately 5 am (0500 hours) prior to the sunrise. Perhaps a street light stimulated him enough to produce his brief bellowing?

"The scissors-grinder cicada" Neotibicen pruinosus pruinosus

The lyric cicadas, Neotibicen lyricen lyricen and the sub-species N. lyricen englehardti, are very distinguishable from the others in both appearance and song. Their calls are a long continuous grinding sound that is mostly heard in the morning and before dusk. They are a beautiful species with a striking array of caramel colored markings on their thorax and teal colored wing veins. The dark lyric, N. lyricen englehardti, is less common and lacks some of the brown patterns.

"The lyric cicada" Neotibicen lyricen lyricen

"The lyric cicada" Neotibicen lyricen lyricen

The lyric cicadas – Neotibicen lyricen lyricen (left) & Lyric cicada spp. comparison (right)

"The dark lyric" Neotibicen lyricen englehardti

"The dark lyric" Neotibicen lyricen englehardti

Linne's cicada, Neotibicen linnei, has a song similar to the swamp cicada only longer and more drawn out. This species can be heard throughout the day.

"Linne's cicada" Neotibicen linnei

As the summer season progresses, the last of these species and the smallest, begin to appear. Neotibicen canicularis or the common "dog day" cicada begins their courtship sounds by mid-August. This species' alias is named after Orion's dog, Sirius, the "Dog Star" that is seen in conjunction with the sun during the period of July 3rd through August 11th. They are commonly associated with pine trees and almost exclusively favor them over all others. They oviposit in dead twigs and cause no real damage to the bark. This in turn doesn't produce any sticky residue leaks that inhibit the nest opening that will later lead to its destruction. The mating signals are a high pitch whine that mirrors the sound of a circular saw. Since this species emerges later than the rest, it is possible to hear them sing into late October and early November; especially during the last remaining warm days of the year.

"The dog day cicada"
Neotibicen canicularis

Shortly upon completion of ecdysis, annual cicadas become strong fliers within hours. They don't require several days for their bodies to harden like it does for periodicals. They only live for a few weeks where they must sing, mate, lay their eggs, and die thereafter.

Swamp cicada teneral adult   *Swamp cicada teneral adult (close up)*

Mating among annual cicadas is rarely encountered in the wild and normally takes place high up in the trees. I have been fortunate enough to stumble upon a few mating pairs over the years that may have erroneously fallen to the ground. If disturbed, they will quickly separate from one another and fly away whereas periodical cicadas will struggle to disengage.

Annual cicadas Neotibicen tibicen
tibicen copulating
(Male: Left) (Female: Right)

Annual cicadas copulating
(Male: Left) (Female: Right)

Annual cicadas copulating
(Male: Right) (Female: Left)

Many annual cicada species prefer to oviposit in dry or dead twigs and seldom leave any visible damage to the vegetation. I've also seen several species (N. tibicen, linnei, and canicularis) oviposit in the bark of trees trunks where again, no evidence of their egg laying is observed. Their eggs can be deposited in early summer or late in the fall when the temperatures may drop low enough to cause them to overwinter. Annual cicadas are also victims to egg parasites that will endanger many of their nests.

Annual cicada ovipositing

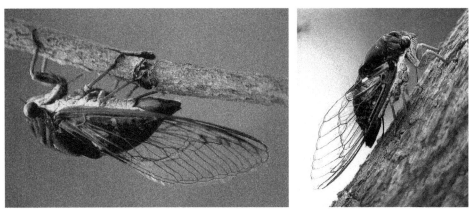

Annual cicada Neotibicen tibicen tibicen ovipositing

Like the periodical cicadas, woodland edges appear to be favored nesting sites rather than the more dense inner forests. As the fall comes to a close, only the exuvia remain. These hollowed shells can be so sturdy that smaller creatures may inhabit them, and some often persist well into the winter months by clinging to the bark far into the following year.

Annual cicada exuvia

IX
CICADA KILLER

Sphecius speciosus

As already mentioned in the "Life Cycle" section on this book, the cicada killer (Sphecius speciosus) is a large digger wasp that specializes in hunting cicadas. They are often seen flying around parks and residential neighborhoods where they appear large enough to carry away your pets or children. But rest assured, unless you're a cicada, they mean you no harm.

However, they like making their burrows in soft, sandy surfaces which can disrupt a perfectly good garden! For those with a green thumb, they can become an annoying distraction! If you come too close to their nesting site, they will give off a threatening buzz and will dart directly at you as a defensive ploy! Otherwise, these wasps are normally timid and will avoid interactions with humans. Only females have stingers and their venom is mild and harmless towards people and animals but is quite paralyzing to a cicada!

Cicada killer burrow

These imposing creatures are 1.5 to 2 inches in length with males being somewhat smaller. Males do not partake in the hunting but feed on nectar. They are fiercely territorial when it comes to females and will engage in battling other males in wrestling contests to win a prospecting mate! Soon after mating, the male dies.

Cicada killer (male)

Cicada killers copulating

*Cicada killers copulating
(Male: Left) (Female: Right)*

Cicada killer (female)

The female wasp hunts cicadas primarily by sight and sound. These wasps begin to appear in July with the majority of their numbers peaking by early August. They fly around and target unsuspecting annual cicadas (Neotibicen spp.). Once a target is acquired, the wasp tackles it and delivers a sting. The sting again merely paralyzes the cicada and renders it helpless. The sting also preserves the cicada's bodily fluids from dehydrating and keeps it alive! Stung cicadas will live longer than those cicadas that live out their normal lives. The wasp will then drag the heavy cicada up the side of a tree or other support and take a short flight with the cicada tucked underneath her body. The weight of the cicada causes the wasp to fly only a short distance at a time and she will have to repeat this step over and over until she reaches her burrow.

Burrow entrance with prey

The burrow is dug out of loose soil and will extend underground at a depth of a foot or more. There is a gravel runway track leading up to the nest opening whose access is about an inch in diameter. The mother wasp removes excess dirt with her jaws or will use her hind legs to kick it free; much like a dog digging a hole to bury a bone. This burrow will have several rounded chambers branching off of the main entrance tunnel. There, the wasp will store the cicada and lay an egg near the thorax of the cicada's body. Unfertilized eggs will develop into males while fertilized eggs will become females. The wasp will already know the sex of the egg and will stock two or more cicadas to a chamber if the egg is female and one cicada if the egg is male. Once the wasp finishes stocking all of the chambers, she will seal off the entrance to the nest. By early September, the adult wasps will have disappeared.

Within several days, the egg will hatch and the wasp larva will begin to feed off the fluids from the cicada's body. The cicada will live through much of this ordeal and will be slowly drained by the larva for almost 2 weeks until only a husk remains. The larva will then spin a thin cocoon around itself where it will remain in the larval stage and overwinter. In spring, the larvae will pupate and emerge from its cocoon during mid-summer. The new wasps will leave the old nests, mate, and the females will dig new burrows to begin the next generation.

X
WHAT IS A LOCUST?

"Differential grasshopper" (female) Melanoplus differentialis

All the while growing up, I had to deal with using the term "locust" to describe a cicada. I studied many insects as a young lad but easily distinguished between the widely different taxon. However, it seemed everyone around me had no idea what a cicada was until I referred to them by their "alias." It was frustrating to me because even my mother referred to them as that until I enlightened her to their proper name.

Luckily that was almost 40 years ago and the times are changing where information/knowledge has become more readily available thanks to the internet and social media. The alias or incorrect term "locust" is slowly becoming a description of the past.

So, what is a locust and how did the name become associated with the cicada?

The name "locust" goes way back to the biblical days where certain species of grasshoppers reproduced too quickly until their numbers became extremely large "swarms." These swarms attacked crops and stripped the foliage clean on all available vegetation. These crops were quickly destroyed and as the creatures moved onward; their numbers were so abundant that as they flew, they resembled a storm cloud advancing on a horizon. Sounds like a thing of a nightmare, right? They definitely were to the people of those older days. These creatures are described in the Bible book of "Exodus" and are one of the 10 plagues that Moses warned the Pharaoh Ramesses would come if he did not let the enslaved Israelites free.

A locust can be any number of species of grasshopper and is not designated to a particular one. It is rather given to any species whose numbers can increase to such enormous "swarm" populations that they become serious pests to agriculture.

The locust name went on for generations throughout human history and eventually into the new world. The year 1633 was the first written account of periodical cicadas meeting the settlers of the Plymouth Colony. Those first immigrants living on the North American shores were not prepared when they first encountered the 17 year cicada. When those cicadas emerged from the ground in massive numbers, the colonists described them as flies and compared them to the locust plagues of the Bible. They had thought these insects had arrived to punish them for something they may have done! The cicada brood involved was probably Brood II which still exists today. However due to descriptive error, the term "locust" was improperly branded on the cicada ever since.

In case you are not familiar with swarming grasshoppers, I will introduce you to a well-known species in the continental United States. This particular species is called the differential grasshopper (Melanoplus differentialis). It is approximately 1.5 to 2 inches in length and is often a tan, green, or brown color. They belong to the insect order, Orthoptera, which also includes katydids and crickets. Females are considerably larger than males and this species has been known to be a serious pest for farmers when their populations increase to a "swarming" status. Thanks to advancements in technology, this nuisance species has been kept mostly in check in modern times but can still become an agricultural threat on occasion.

"Differential grasshopper" (female) Melanoplus differentialis

The life cycle of this insect is very simple. Their eggs are laid in soil just below the surface. After mating, a female grasshopper will thrust her abdomen between crevices and lay between 40 to 200 eggs in a protective egg mass. These egg nests will overwinter and the young nymphs will hatch the following late spring. Farmers destroy many of these nests by simply plowing their fields.

After hatching and exiting their underground burrow (or nest), the nymphs, which slightly resemble small versions of their adult forms minus the wings, will immediately begin seeking food. They have chewing mouth parts and when plentiful, can easily strip a plant of its leaves. As the nymphs feed, they will go through several nymphal stages, thus shedding their exoskeletal skins and thereby grow a little larger each time. As they grow, the more they continue to feed. The nymphs grow very rapidly and can mature in approximately one to two months! After reaching maturity, they will mate and again lay their eggs in soil, repeating the process. Like any other fast producing herbivore, they can quickly become a serious pest and will eat many different types of plant species.

There is normally only one generation per year.

XI
WHERE AND HOW
TO FIND CICADAS

Perhaps some of you are wondering how I obtain most of my cicada photographs or simply would like to observe this wonderful insect up close? Well, here are some tips for the amateur huntsman who does not have a profession set up or insect traps.

LOCATING THE PERIODICAL "MAGIC" CICADA

Periodical cicadas

Locating members of this genus is actually very easy. There are no tricks involved at all. Merely check out the brood maps located in this book and they will give you the approximate when and where they will appear. Or you can check your local news outlets and the internet for announcements on their whereabouts because the media is sure to alert those who are having bug anxieties!

These insects make for intriguing headlines. They have been known to cause vehicle accidents especially when a panicked driver has one land in their lap due to an open car window! Back in the late eighties, a cicada was used to frighten away a restaurant employee so the culprit could take money from the cash register. People react to them in different ways and reading comments in social media is frequently entertaining! Their coming is either praised or the harbinger of the apocalypse!

If you are in/or near an emergence area... Not to worry, they won't be hard to find! Simply follow the constant sound to the nearest woodlands and you'll find thousands, perhaps millions all at once! Talk about cicada overload, ah? These cicadas prefer forest clearings which is where you'll find the majority of their population. They always appear in large numbers in order to satiate predators and can be found on the ground, on fences, grasses, houses, and especially in trees.

Since periodical cicadas are "predator foolhardy," they won't be hard to collect. Most occasions you can walk right up to them and pick them up. A male cicada may cause a scene when he responds with disapproval!

If the first one you see flies away don't be discouraged, that's just their instinct for survival. Cicadas are like people, some are smarter than others. Keep looking, there will be more. And remember, periodical cicadas begin appearing in late April to early May in the Southern states and late May to early June in the Northern states. Once they start emerging, they will be around for approximately six weeks....

LOCATING THE ANNUAL CICADA

Annual cicada teneral adult

Annual cicadas can be a real challenge! They are found across much of the country and begin appearing in late June and will continue to emerge into September. Annual cicadas are NOT predator foolhardy like their periodic cousins. When threatened, they take off in a hurry! There were times I accidentally stumbled across a male as he sounded his alarm and took to the wing.

Annual cicadas are noisy flyers and clumsy when it comes to landing. When they flap their wings, the sound reminds me of playing card stuck in the spokes of a bicycle. When they come to a suitable tree, they can be heard crashing through the smaller twigs before resting on a branch. They apparently don't believe in evasive maneuvers.

At the beginning of this book, I described my escapades as a youth by climbing a tree where a male was singing. I moved very slowly for if I was too quick, I would startle him. Once I was within several feet of the insect, I would wait patiently. While the male sings, he usually walks about in between notes. When the cicada crawled within reach, I would cup my hands and lash out. 50% of the time I was successful in catching them with my bare hands despite the creature's awful screeching indicating his displeasure.

If you absolutely have to climb trees, use a standard butterfly net. However, I wouldn't suggest climbing trees at all. This method can be extremely dangerous and possibly cause serious injury if you fall. I recommend you DO NOT CLIMB THE TREES!

Sometimes species sit and sing on smaller trees and lower vegetation. If you hunt for them using a long handled butterfly net, remember to MOVE VERY SLOW. Slow movements will not startle them. Just inch towards them a little at a time and you will be rewarded by your patience.

The best method in locating annuals is by catching them prior to or just after they emerge from their last nymphal skin. Pine trees are a favorite host for some species, so check in neighborhoods where older pine trees are located.

Annual cicadas have adapted well to city life, so finding them in towns won't be too hard. Also check in areas such as parks or cemeteries where the older trees are virtually undisturbed. You'll probably find the best emergence there.

Like most species, annual cicadas generally emerge at night when their predators are the least active. Most cities and cemeteries prohibit night time visitors, therefore I suggest you hunt those that emerge after 5:00 pm (1700 hours) or during the very early morning after sunrise. Rarely will they emerge during the mid-afternoon. The closer to nightfall, the better are your chances of locating a nymph crawling across the ground or one clinging to a tree trunk ready to molt.

Check under trees where their shells are found in good numbers or on trees where you've seen them the year before. Annuals are often repeat visitors year after year and since their emergence is staggered over the summer, keep checking daily and nightly... Chances are more will emerge under this same tree over the next few weeks.

A great time to hunt would be after it rained or when the ground is damp. Nymphs seem to emerge better when the ground is moist and their emergence holes become more apparent.

And lastly, you may want to inspect parking lots early in the morning that are illuminated at night; especially those positioned in proximity to populated woodlands. Cicadas are attracted to bright lights overnight and can be found resting on the ground at the crack of dawn. The more the sun and temperatures rise, the less likely you'll find them since they'll eventually return to the trees. Remember that old saying? "The early bird catches the worm."

Do NOT disturb a cicada if their molting process has already begun. Outside interference can prevent the cicada from molting successfully, cause deformities on the insect's body, or even death. This is a very delicate moment in the cicada's life, please appreciate their beauty and be patient. Once their wings expand and dry, you'll have a perfect specimen. Like other cicada species, they won't be strong flyers for a couple of hours. So don't be careless in your handling of them at this vulnerable stage.

If you locate a nymph crawling across the ground, be gentle and pick it up. Place it on a tree or a firm plant and watch it molt before your very eyes! It's a captivating sight to behold! If you must go hunting at night, use a bright flash light. A teneral adult's pale body and glossy wings will reflect the light and be very pronounced.

XII
CICADAS AS FOOD

Yes, that's right. Some people may cringe at the thought of this, but cicadas can be an excellent source of protein which contains no fat for those watching their weight or counting calories. They are indeed edible.

The Native Americans were eating them long before the white man settled these shores. Asian countries serve them in fancy restaurants where they are considered a delicacy.

If you like shrimp or lobster, I personally don't see a huge transition from sea food to insects. Someone once referred to them as "land shrimp." I chuckled upon hearing that description for the first time, but he definitely had the right idea. He informed me he would find them in the act of ecdysis, gather them up, remove their wings and legs, and then boil them before serving them with cocktail sauce. The thought of it sounded appetizing!

I have eaten them myself. Granted, I still prefer the taste of sea food but if prepared right, they could make for a hearty meal.

There are plenty of recipes across the internet and books on how to cook them, so I won't go into detail here. I have seen them cooked into a stir fry, skewered on sticks, boiled and eaten like shrimp, deep fried, baked in cookies, and blended into ice cream. Yum! Aren't you hungry yet?

A WORD OF CAUTION…. Studies have found that some specimens of periodical cicada gathered from places treated with pesticides and herbicides contained mercury toxins!

XIII
HOW TO DETER OR DESTROY CICADAS:

DETERRENCE

Annual cicadas are almost never found in large numbers to raise any major concern. An annual cicada's egg laying process is nowhere near the destructiveness to that of the Magicicada races despite their larger size. In fact, I've inspected fresh Neotibicen egg nests up close and I was barely able to notice them! If I hadn't discovered a female ovipositing, I would have never noticed these nests at all.

Periodical cicadas cause very noticeable damage due to their massive numbers. The slits they leave in the wood are easy to find and cause "flagging;" where the leaves and branches turn brown and die.

My suggestion is to note the emergence years in your area and do not plant trees or shrubs on those years. Especially orchard growers since periodicals like fruit trees! If you absolutely must plant on these years, please wait until after mid-July when their emergence and egg laying is completed. If you already have established saplings, cover them with a cheese cloth prior to their expected arrival and tie the cloth near the base of the tree. This will prevent females from ovipositing that causes the damage.

Placing materials or obstructions such as tape around the base of your trees is usually a waste of your time. It may prevent some emerging nymphs from molting on the trunk but they'll just relocate to another object.

HOW TO DESTROY CICADAS

There are many chemical agents that kill the cicada. By applying these agents will not only kill cicadas, but will endanger or kill other beneficial insects and animals as well! Damage caused by cicada oviposition is a natural pruning that eliminates weaker branches. Please do not use insecticides that may do more harm than good and pollute the environment. Periodical cicadas are only around for approximately six weeks, ordinarily ONCE every 13 or 17 years!

My suggestion is simply to LEAVE THEM ALONE! Try to enjoy this natural phenomenon. This information is for general reference. Please remember that cicadas are harmless. I will say this over and over again; they do not sting, bite, or carry diseases. And yes, I do know what chemical agents are used in their destruction... However, I won't tell you! I love these insects and have the highest respect for nature and our environment. Have the common courtesy to do the same....

XIV
CICADAS AND THE FUTURE

Brood X Emergence – Spring Grove Cemetery, Cincinnati, Ohio 2004

1999 and 2016 were extraordinary years for the cicada, especially in Ohio. Periodical cicadas appeared by the millions and the annual cicadas followed suite by appearing in the thousands during the latter half of the summers. However, I fear years such as these may become only a memory, provided if things don't change over the next 50 to 100 years.

Cicadas have many natural enemies... Birds, spiders, snakes, mites, small mammals, parasites, fungi, and wasps... But none of these creatures are ever enough to totally eradicate an entire colony or species. In fact, it is these predators that help keep the natural balance in the cycle of life. There is only one predator that constantly likes to upset this balance and wants to control it to meet its demands... That predator is a primate known as "MAN."

Mankind is the only predator in the world that destroys what it doesn't understand, manipulates to meet his/her will, and often has little regard for any other living thing other than him/herself. With each passing year, there is new pollution entering the atmosphere and water, and forests are cut down in order to make room for human development.

Once where tall trees have stood, are now replaced my monuments of steel and glass. Humanity is the only species on the planet whose population is running rampant with nothing to preserve the balance. The majority of this planet's forests and undisturbed areas are expected to disappear within the next 40 to 50 years. Once the forests are gone, so will many species of plants and animals. Some are still unidentified by scientists today... Some of which we may never learn ever existed.

Human negligence is another key factor in the downfall of the cicada. For example, an introduced species known as the gypsy moth (Lymantria dispar) has spread westward from a small portion of the New England states to a range that nearly includes the entire Eastern Time zone in less than a century. These moths multiply and appear in great numbers that rival the colonies of the periodical cicada. The moths are destructive since their larvae can completely defoliate many acres of trees. Years of continuous feeding will eventually kill the host trees they inhabit and increase competition with periodical cicadas over the same food sources.

There is also the introduction of the English or house sparrow (Passer domesticus) during the 1850's. These birds have spread across the country and have decimated remnants of Magicicada colonies that were already competing with human encroachment. This sparrow is not only aggressive, but can be a serious pest to others creatures and people. These birds feed on grain, cause damage with their droppings, carry many diseases, and most of all, they compete with and have caused the decline of several native bird populations.

In more recent years, many ash trees across the Eastern and mid-Western states had to be cut down and the wood destroyed due to an invasive species known as the emerald ash borer beetle (Agrilus planipennis).

Another example of human negligence would be the spread of forest fires often caused by utter carelessness. Ignorance destroys many cicadas and other creatures.

Not all cicada species have suffered from human development. Many species of annual cicadas have become accustomed to living under man's feet. Annuals seem to fare well alongside urbanization.

Unfortunately, this isn't the case for every species. The periodical cicada has suffered immensely and its range has diminished greatly over the past century and continues to do so. Periodical cicadas seldom frequent cities like the annual cicadas and prefer woodland dwellings. There are organizations trying to preserve areas for cicadas and other animals but such efforts maybe a sad case of too little, too late.

Entire broods once noted historically have gone extinct. Even in Ohio, the ranges of its five existing broods are shrinking due to human intrusion and habitat loss.

What is the eventual fate of the cicada? Unless something drastic is done, their numbers will continue to decline. Even though periodicals appear by the millions during designated brood years, they are in fact...A THREATENED SPECIES!!!

Many people may disagree or ignore this fact, but please...OPEN YOUR EYES!

If you compare historical records, you can easily see what I'm talking about. Once you make this comparison of the past hundred years, think forward to a future projection for the next century. With human populations constantly on the rise, do you honestly think the brood ranges will remain the same?

The time to act is now... Otherwise an American heritage such as the periodical cicada that is found nowhere else in the world will become a part of American history. Please always keep in mind...Extinction is forever....

Only after the last tree has been cut down, only after the last river has been poisoned, only after the last fish has been caught, only then you will find that money cannot be eaten. - CREE INDIAN PROPHECY (Author Unknown)

*Brood X Emergence – Spring Grove
Cemetery, Cincinnati, Ohio 2004*

XV
GLOSSARY

Abdomen -The posterior part of the body behind the thorax.

Aggregations- A large group or mass composed of many individuals.

Antennae - A pair of flexible segmented sensory appendages on the head of an insect.

Arthropod - Invertebrate animals that have an exoskeleton, a segmented body, and jointed appendages.

Arthropoda –The phylum or group that comprises of arthropods.

Aphid - Numerous tiny soft-bodied insects that suck sap from the stems and leaves of plants, can reproduce rapidly, and are often agricultural pests.

Auchenorrhyncha– The suborder of insects from the Hemiptera that contains most of the familiar members of what was once called the Homoptera, such as the cicada. This group of organisms consists of having mouth parts designed for piercing and sucking plant fluids.

Biology –The science of studying life and living organisms.

Biotic Community - This is a group of interacting organisms living within a particular habitat or region.

Brood - A number of offspring produced or hatched at the same time.

Cicada - An insect often with a long life cycle that has a stout body, wide blunt head, and two sets of transparent wings. The males have two vibrating membranes on their abdomens that produce sound.

Cicadidae -The family of insects comprising of cicadas.

Cicadoidea –The super family of insects in the order Hemiptera, consisting of the family Cicadidae.

Chorusing Centers– When groups of male cicadas sing together in trees.

Copulation - Sexual intercourse.

Ecdysis - The shedding of the outer layer of skin or exoskeleton by an insect as it grows or matures.

Ectoparasite - A parasite that lives on the skin but not within the body.

Emergence - The process of coming into view after being concealed.

Entomologist - A person whose expertise is in the branch of zoology involving insects.

Entomology - The scientific study of insects.

Exoskeleton - The hard outer external skeleton of an insect that provides structure and protection.

Exuvia - The remains of an exoskeleton that are left after an insect has molted.

Exuviae - The plural form of the word, exuvia.

Fauna – Animal life of a particular region or habitat.

Flagging – When tree limbs are weakened by cicada nests and resemble flags in the wind after breakage occurs.

Flora - Plant life of a particular region or habitat.

Fossorial Foreleg – An insect's front leg designed for digging.

Genera – The plural form of the word, genus.

Genus - A class or group of living or extinct animals or plants with similar attributes or features.

Hadoa - This is the genus of Cicadidae inhabiting Western North America.

Head - The front part of the body that contains the brain, mouth, and many of the important sensory organs.

Hemiptera – The order of insect groups also known as "true bugs" comprising of the cicadas, aphids, planthoppers, leafhoppers, spittlebugs, and shield bugs.

Homoptera – The obsolete suborder of order Hemiptera.

Honeydew - A sticky clear liquid that is often secreted by cicadas when they feed on plant fluids.

Hybrid - The offspring of two animals from different species.

Hybridization - The process of mating organisms of different species to create a hybrid or mixed offspring.

Imago - Adult stage of an insect.

Insect - The class of invertebrates that have an exoskeleton, three body parts (head, thorax and abdomen), six legs, and two antennae.

Insecta - The class comprising of the insects.

Instar - A stage in the life of an insect between two periods of molts.

Labium - A mouth part or fused appendages forming a lip-like device in insects.

Locust – A type of grasshopper that can form large swarms which become agricultural pests.

Magicicada – A genus of cicada, also known as periodical cicadas, that appear in large numbers with a life span normally stemming 13 or 17 years.

Mandibles - Mouth organs of insects used for seizing food.

Massospora - A fungus that infects Magicicada species by filling the insect's abdomen with spores thereby destroys their ability to reproduce.

Maxillae - Appendages located behind the mandibles of insects.

Megapomponia - A genus of cicada, from Southeast Asia, that contains the world's largest cicada species.

Mesothorax - The middle segment of the thorax of an insect, bearing the middle legs and the anterior wings.

Molting – The process of shedding an outer covering, such as an exoskeleton, which is then replaced by new growth.

Morphology - The study of the form and structure of animals.

Mortality - The state or condition of one day having to die.

Naturalist - A person who studies and appreciates nature.

Neotibicen - A genus of cicada, also known as annual or dog day cicadas, that appear every summer in Eastern North America with an approximate life span of 2 to 5 years.

Nymph - An immature form of an insect that does not change greatly and somewhat resembles its adult stage as it grows.

Okanagana - A genus of cicada which sometimes appears in large numbers and mistaken for periodical cicadas.

Organism - A living thing.

Ovipositor -A tubular organ female insects use to lay their eggs.

Oviposit - To lay eggs.

Ovipositing - Laying eggs.

Parasite - An organism that lives in or on another host organism for nourishment while offering no benefit in return.

Phylum - A major category of living organisms whose taxonomic rank is below kingdom and above class in the biological classifications.

Predator Foolhardiness – When animals fail to avoid a predator despite the apparent danger or imminent death.

Predator Satiation – When animals are so abundant that their numbers overwhelm their predators thus allowing enough of them to reproduce since their enemies can't consume them all.

Prothorax - The anterior segment of an insect's thorax that doesn't bear any wings.

Relict Population - A species that inhabits a much smaller geographic area than it did in the past due to changes in their environment.

Rostrum - A beak like mouth part some insects have that they use to suck plant fluids.

Species - A group of living things that share common characteristics and are capable of producing fertile offspring.

Straggling – When periodical cicadas emerge either a year or more too soon or too late from their particular brood.

Synchronized - Happening at the same time.

Taxon - Any group or unit in biological classification which related organisms are classified.

Teneral - A state of the imago or adult insect immediately after molting during which it has a soft exoskeleton and pale coloring.

Thorax - The middle section of an insect's body between the head and the abdomen that bares the legs and wings.

Tibicen – A former genus name whose species are now divided into the Hadoa and Neotibicen in North America.

Trachea - The tract or air-conveying tubes of the respiratory system.

Tymbals - An abdominal membrane that vibrates and forms part of the sound-producing organs.

Xylem - Tissue in vascular plants whose function is to transport water and nutrients from the roots to the leaves.

Zoologist - A scientist who studies animals.

Zoology - The scientific study of animals and animal life.

Periodical cicada

XVI
INTERNET RESOURCES

Here is a list of my favorite cicada websites. Please take note that the following were functioning webpages at the time of this publication.

Bug Guide: www.bugguide.net
Cicada Central: http://hydrodictyon.eeb.uconn.edu/projects/cicada/cc.php
Cicada Mania: www.cicadamania.com
Cicadas of Michigan: http://insects.ummz.lsa.umich.edu/fauna/Michigan_Cicadas/Michigan/Index.html
Great Lakes Cicada Page: www.magicicada.net
Magicicada Central: www.magicicada.org
Massachusetts Cicadas: www.masscic.org
Songs of Insects: http://songsofinsects.com

XVII
REFERENCES &
RECOMMENDED READING

Alexander, R. D., and T. E. Moore. 1962. The evolutionary relationships of 17-year and 13-year cicadas, and three new species (Homoptera, Cicadidae, Magicicada).Univ. of Mich. Mus. Zool. Misc. Pub. 121: 1-59.

Bulmer, M.G. 1977. Periodical insects. Am. Nat. 111: 1099-1117

Dybas, H.S., and D. D. Davis. 1962. A population census of seventeen-year periodical cicadas (Homoptera: Cicadidae: Magicicada). Ecology 43: 432-444.

Dybas, H.S., and M. Lloyd. 1962. Isolation by habitat in two synchronized species of periodical cicadas (Homoptera: Cicadidae: Magicicada). Ecology 43: 444-459.

Eaton, E. and K. Kaufman. 2007. Kaufman Field Guide to Insects of North America. Houghton Mifflin Co. 392 pp.

Elliott, L. and W. Hershberger. 2007. The Songs of Insects. Houghton Mifflin Co. 228 pp.

Heath, J. E.1968. Thermal synchronization of emergence in periodical "17-year"cicadas (Homoptera: Cicadidae: Magicicada). Am. Midl. Nat. 80: 440-447.

Hill, K. B.R; D. C. Marshall, M. S. Moulds & C. Simon. 2015. Molecular phylogenetics, diversification, and systematics of Tibicen Latreille 1825 and allied cicadas of the tribe Cryptotympanini, with three new genera and emphasis on species from the USA and Canada (Hemiptera: Auchenorrhyncha: Cicadidae) Zootaxa 3985 (2): 219–251.

Hutchins,Ross E. 1971. The Cicada. Addison-Wesley. 48 pp.

Irwin, M.D., and J. R. Coelho. 2000. Distribution of the Iowan Brood of Periodical Cicadas (Homoptera: Cicadidae: Magicicada spp.) in Illinois. Ann. Entomol. Soc. Amer.93: 82- 89.

Karban, R.1984. Opposite density effects of nymphal and adult mortality for periodical cicadas (Magicicada spp.). Ecology 65: 1656-1661.

Koenig, W.,& Liebhold, A. 2005. Effects of periodical cicada emergences on abundance and synchrony of avian populations. Ecology, 86 (7), 1873-1882.

Koenig, W.,& Liebhold, A. 2003. Regional impacts of periodical cicadas on oak radial increment. Can. J. For. Res. 33: 1084–1089.

Kritsky, G.1999. In Ohio's Backyard: Periodical Cicadas. Ohio Biological Survey: Backyard Series No. 2; 83 pp.

Kritsky, G.2004. Periodical Cicadas: The Plague and the Puzzle. Indiana Academy of Science. 147 pp.

Lee, Y.J. 2016. Description of three new genera, Paratibicen, Gigatibicen, and Ameritibicen, of Cryptotympanini (Hemiptera: Cicadidae) and a key to their species Journal of Asia-Pacific Biodiversity, Volume 9, Issue 4, 1 December 2016, Pages 448–454.

Lehmann-Ziebarth, N., Heideman, P., Shapiro, R., Stoddart, S., Hsiao, C., Stephenson, G.,Milewski, P., & Ives, A. 2005. Evolution of Periodicity in Periodical Cicadas. Ecology, 86 (12), 3200-3211.

Lloyd, M.1987. A successful rearing of 13-year periodical cicadas beyond their present range and beyond that of 17-year cicadas. Am. Midl. Nat. 117: 362-368.

Marlatt, C.L. 1898. The Periodical Cicada. An account of Cicada septendecim, its natural enemies and the mean of preventing its injury. USDA Div. Entomol. Bull. 14 (New Series). Washington: Government Printing Office. 148 pp.

Marlatt, C.L. 1907. The periodical cicada. U.S.D.A. Bur. Entomol. Bull. 71: 1-181.

Marshall, D.C., J. R. Cooley, R. D. Alexander, and T. E. Moore. 1996. New records of Michigan Cicadidae (Homoptera), with notes on the use of songs to monitor range changes. Great Lakes Entomologist 29: 165-169.

Moulds, M.S. 1990. Australian cicadas. Kensington, NSW, Australia: NSWU Press. 217 pp.

Myers, J. G.1929. Insect singers; a natural history of the cicadas. London, G. Routledge and Sons, limited. 304 pp.

Rodenhouse, N. L., P. J. Bohlen, and G. W. Barrett. 1997. Effects of woodland shape on the spatial distribution and density of 17-year periodical cicadas (Homoptera: Cicadidae). Am. Midl. Nat. 137: 124-135.

Riley, C. V.1885. The periodical cicada. An account of Cicada septendecim and its tredecim race, with a chronology of all broods known. USDA Div. of Entomol. Bulletin 8: 1-46, 2nd ed.

Russell, L.M., and M. B. Stoetzel. 1991. Inquilines in egg nests of periodical cicadas (Homoptera: Cicadidae). Proc. Entomol. Soc. Wash. 93: 480-488.

Sanborn, A.F. Catalogue of the Cicadoidea (Hemiptera: Auchenorrhyncha). 2013. With contributions to the bibliography by Martin H. Villet. Elsevier. Inc., Academic Press, San Diego. 1001 pp.

Sanborn, A.F., and M.S. Heath. 2013. Catalogue of the cicadas (Hemiptera: Cicadoidea: Cicadidae) of continental North America North of Mexico. Thomas Say Monographs of the Entomological Society of America. Entomological Society of America, Lanham, MD. 227 pp.

Sanborn, A.F., and M.S. Heath. 2016. Megatibicen n. gen., a new North American cicada genus (Hemiptera: Cicadidae: Cicadinae: Cryptotympanini). Zootaxa Vol. 4168, No 3.

Sanborn, A.F. and P. K. Phillips. 2013. Biogeography of the Cicadas (Hemiptera: Cicadidae) of North America, North of Mexico. Diversity: 5, 166-239.

Shian, D. 2008. Cicada: Exotic Views. Hebei Fine Arts Publishing House. 87 pp.

Simon, C.,R. Karban, and M. Lloyd. 1981. Patchiness, density, and aggregative behavior in sympatric allochronic populations of 17-year cicadas. Ecology 62: 1525-1535.

Snodgrass, R. E. 1921. The seventeen year locust. Smithson. Inst. Annu. Rep. for 1919, pp. 381-409. Publ. 2607. Gov. Print. Off., Wash. D.C.

Soper, R.,A. J. Delyzer, and L. F. R. Smith. 1976. The genus Massospora entomopathogenic for cicadas. Part II. Biology of Massospora levispora and its host Okanagana rimosa, with notes on Massospora cicadina on the periodical cicadas. Ann. Entomol. Soc. Am. 69: 89-95.

Wheeler, G., Williams, K., & Smith, K. (1992). Role of periodical cicadas (Homoptera: Cicadidae: Magicicada) in forest nutrient cycles Forest Ecology and Management,51 (4), 339-346.

White, J. 1980. Resource partitioning by ovipositing cicadas. Am. Nat. 115: 1-28.

White, J., and M. Lloyd. 1975. Growth rates of 17- and 13-year periodical cicadas. Am.Midl. Nat. 94: 127-143.

White, J., and M. Lloyd. 1979. 17-year cicadas emerging after 18 years: a new brood? Evolution 33: 1193-1199.

White, J., and M. Lloyd. 1981. On the stainability and mortality of periodical cicada eggs. Am. Midl. Nat. 106: 219-228.

White, J., M. Lloyd, and J. H. Zar. 1979. Faulty eclosion in crowded suburban periodical cicadas: Populations out of control. Ecology 60: 305-315.

Williams, K.S., and C. Simon. 1995. The ecology, behavior, and evolution of periodical cicadas. Annu. Rev. Entomol. 40: 269-295.

Williams, K.S., K. G. Smith, and F. M. Stephen. 1993. Emergence of 13-yr periodical cicadas (Cicadidae: Magicicada): phenology, mortality, and predator satiation. Ecology 74: 1143-1152.

Yang, Louie H; 2006. Periodical cicadas use light for oviposition site selection. Proc Biol Sci. 273(1604):2993–3000.

CPSIA information can be obtained
at www.ICGtesting.com
Printed in the USA
BVHW021942151021
619064BV00005B/28